GLASGOW'S GODFATHER

GLASGOW'S GODFATHER

**THE ASTONISHING INSIDE STORY OF
WALTER NORVAL, THE CITY'S FIRST CRIME BOSS**

ROBERT JEFFREY

BLACK & WHITE PUBLISHING

First published in 2003
This edition first published 2011
by Black & White Publishing Ltd
29 Ocean Drive, Edinburgh EH6 6JL

1 3 5 7 9 10 8 6 4 2   11 12 13 14 15

ISBN 978 1 84502 348 5

A CIP catalogue record for this book
is available from the British Library.

Typeset by RefineCatch Limited, Bungay, Suffolk
Printed and bound by CPI Cox & Wyman, Reading

CONTENTS

ACKNOWLEDGEMENTS

I would like to thank Marie Jeffrey, Dr Grant Jeffrey, Samantha Boyd, Ian Watson, Dr Stuart Jeffrey, Maris Thomson, John Watson, Nick Dastoor, Jean McKinnon, Walter Norval and his family (particularly his daughter Rita) and friends, and the staff of the Glasgow Room in the Mitchell Library for their assistance in the production of this book.

RJ
Carradale, Argyll

1

THE BOY CALLED KID MILLIONS

It is a haunting image. Late on a dark winter evening, from a window in a top-floor tenement flat, a child of barely five looks out across the street. Immediately opposite, down below on ground level, there are bright lights and the sound of glasses clinking and men talking loudly. There is also, on a regular basis, the sight of blood on the streets, the sound of men fighting, mostly with bare fists, sometimes with a broken bottle in their hand, as they spill out after some dispute or other inside the pub. The child watches.

The pub was Scott's in Garscube Road, a stretch of tenement landscape known to its often lawless denizens as the High Road. Nearby was Glasgow's infamous Twilight Zone. It was the early thirties. The child was Walter Norval. In the fullness of time, he grew up to rule the dark oppressive streets he looked down on as a child. And more. He became King of the Twilight Zone. A man feared and respected on the streets, a self-styled 'fighting man', one of the most infamous armed robbers in British criminal history and a man prepared to spill blood with alarming regularity. The first of a succession of Glasgow gangland Godfathers.

The journey, from a wide-eyed and lonely boy, who grew up with too much time on his hands, too much imagination and too little control, to big league criminal is a violent, complex and bloody story – but a story not without humour.

* * *

Drive west out of Glasgow city centre along Garscube Road today and you pick up no hint of the remarkable past of this area and its place in Glasgow's history. A petrol station, a modern health centre, some industrial premises, a warehouse or two, the odd pub, a couple of bookie's shops and before you know it you are on your way to the wide avenues leading out of the city to Loch Lomond and the Highlands. It is forgettable and bland, no different from a hundred roads in a hundred British towns or cities.

It was not always like this. Once it was lined with smoke-blackened dark tenements seething with families, dozens of pubs, old fashioned grocers and wine shops. The tramcars, to and from the city centre, rattled past pawnbrokers, brothels, dance halls, snooker parlours and what passed for night clubs in those days. Street bookies stood in back courts collecting 'lines' – scraps of paper with various wagers scrawled on them – and paying out to lucky punters. It was a favourite place for theatrical digs for the comics, singers and exotic dancers who filled the bills in the variety halls just a tram ride away in the city centre. It had a somewhat bohemian air. And, being Glasgow, it also had more than its share of street fighters and gangs.

Walter Norval, the man who became one of the hardest of the hard men, was born just the throw of a knife blade away from the Garscube Road, in Ferguson Street, on a bitter February night in 1928. And, for more than seventy years, he spent his life, when not in jail – which was for many long years – in the area. Today he lives just a few hundred yards away from the scene of his most infamous exploits. Now in his eighties, he looks down on the Glasgow gangland scene, from his comfortable home, for more than twenty years, still 'up a close' in Maryhill.

There is a choice of approach – either from leafy Cleveden Road off Great Western Road, with its rows of beautiful villas or terraced houses and immaculately kept gardens, or from the altogether tougher Maryhill Road. A major feature of Maryhill

Road is the stout stone walls of the old Maryhill Barracks where some of Scotland's hard men in army uniform – the legendary and much feared 'poison dwarfs', as the post-war Germans christened the Scottish soldiers of the Rhine Army – were once billeted. A police station is another much-needed local landmark. The area where Walter now lives has some of the dereliction of Glasgow sink schemes, like Barrowfield in the East End or some of the streets around Ibrox Stadium, where neatly kept windows sit side by side with homes that are boarded up, their walls scorched with flame marks.

Within yards of his home, Walter can point out the scene of a drug tragedy – iron plates now hiding a burnt-out interior where a drug addict died a desperate and lonely death. A few yards away, a close mouth is the site of a fatal shooting – just another episode in the endless turf wars over the control of Glasgow's drug scene. These wars have continued into the twenty-first century and the shootings on the streets are recorded regularly and in gory blood-stained detail by the city's tabloids.

Walter's own flat is spotless and well cared for – the walls and bookcases crammed with Celtic Football Club memorabilia and videos. Celtic are, of course, the Catholic half of Glasgow's famous football rivals, the so-called 'Old Firm'. Walter calls himself a Protestant and would, in the normal order of things in this divided city, be expected to be a Rangers supporter. But, surprisingly, Celtic, in particular, carry a fair share of supporters who have crossed the religious divide – perhaps because, in the old days, the club was slightly less religiously exclusive. In 1967, when managed by a Protestant, the legendary Jock Stein, Celtic became the first British team to win the European Cup. These days, both parts of the Old Firm have players of both faiths – or none – on their books. So Walter continues a lifelong love for Celtic's green and white hoops and the walls of his home, where he is seen photographed in the company of some of the great players, offer testimony to his support.

The folk in such an area welcome a Godfather as a neighbour. No liberties are taken when Walter Norval is around. Indeed, when he moved in, there was a little bother with pot-smoking kids littering the steps outside the house. Clearing up that problem was easy for Walter and his connections.

Walter's successors as Glasgow Godfather have sometimes taken to living in vast villas surrounded by high-tech security, far from the homes of the people whose lives they have blighted. That is not the Norval style. Life up a Glasgow close is fine for him. He may have contempt for the flash lifestyle of the new crooks but he reserves his full contempt for their actions. To him the current Godfathers, and the wannabes in the wings, are little more than 'grocers' – shopkeepers whose stalls sell misery and despair to the victims on the streets. Drug dealing is anathema to this man who had a spectacular and violent career in crime. He remembers the comments of a local legal eagle of some repute who remarked, when Walter was sent down to Peterhead for fourteen years for armed robbery in November 1977, that the gang scene in Glasgow would change forever with his removal from the streets. The lawyer was right. With Walter, armed robbery was the driving force. After him, drugs became the main interest of the gangs. And they still are. Recent drug wars have seen men shot down in busy streets in daylight.

Glasgow, in the twenty-first century, has reinvented itself with pavement café culture and world-class museums, theatre and music. Its renaissance is real and admired round the world – indeed, its regeneration is taken as a model for other cities. And not just in Britain. But, like any city of similar size, there is an inevitable evil underbelly of crime which feeds off the modern appetite for a chemically fuelled escape from reality – an appetite that seems as strong in yuppie businessmen and women – as it is in the folk who live a life surrounded by illegal moneylenders, dole queues and squalid housing. In his late years, Walter Norval, a grandfather many times over, played a role in the battle against drugs. But we are getting ahead of ourselves and all that is a matter for much later in this book.

What made Walter Norval into the man he became? There is huge scope for the ongoing nature versus nurture debate in his remarkable life. What is sure is that he is rich, red dripping meat for any psychologist with an interest in the forming of the criminal personality. Though it is interesting to note that, during his many years in prison and despite behaviour that, on occasion, could only be described as psychotic, he has had minimal contact with psychologists – something that is a mark of his time. Today, he would be analysed in great detail – his upbringing, his motivation and his every thought given intense professional white-coated scrutiny.

As a toddler, he was growing up in a city that Sir Percy Sillitoe, the legendary chief constable of Glasgow, described, at that time, as being overrun with gangs terrorising decent citizens and waging war between themselves in the streets. Sillitoe was the man largely credited with beating the pre-war gangs by meeting force with force. He assembled a ruthless bunch of hard cops, The Untouchables, as hard as the hardest of the neds, and set about knocking the gangs into submission with fist and baton. My book, *Gangs of Glasgow*, chronicles his success in some detail but points out the cyclical nature of gang warfare. The bad guys keep bouncing back – something even Walter Norval admits. It would have been interesting to see how Sir Percy would have coped with Norval when he was at his peak as a gang overlord in the sixties and seventies. A wily thinker and planner, he was a criminal of a different stripe from those who blighted the Glasgow scene in the twenties and thirties – but he was just as handy with a knife or gun.

After the Second World War, the phrase 'latchkey kid' came into vogue to describe kids who came home from school to pick up the key from under the front door mat and let themselves into empty houses. Dad would be out at work as would mum and both denied their kids companionship in order to secure a joint income large enough to finance a mortgage and maybe a fortnight or so abroad each summer. The home – rather the house – would, perhaps, be on a modern estate, with comfortable, trendy furniture, a record player and a television set, but it could be a lonely and empty place for long hours. The latchkey kid was a phenomenon much discussed in the papers and on radio and television.

There is a fascination with the idea of the child who largely brings him- or herself up with minimal parental control. Hollywood even gets in on the act with films like those in the *Home Alone* series and, to this day, the red top tabloids revel in finding tales of youngsters left to fend for themselves while the parents party in the sunshine of Majorca or wherever. But this is nothing new. Walter Norval spent most of his formative years fending for himself – thieving for survival almost from the day his nappies were removed. Stealing was a conscienceless act and remorse was an emotion never experienced. Though, in an interesting aside, he claims never to have been a burglar or to have stolen from his own kind – only shops, banks and businesses! But that he did in spades!

In literature and films, gangsters' mothers are always a lurking presence and, to greater or lesser extents, they influence the way their sons' criminal minds develop. Walter's mother Eva was an interesting, entrepreneurial character. As a thirteen-year-old, she would buy a crate of oranges and sell them round the tenements – 'Sweet Sevilles – three a penny'. Later in life, with Walter just months old, she lost a child, Billy, when he was knocked down by a Glasgow Corporation bus in Renfrew Street in 1928. A modest sum, paid in compensation, went towards starting a room-and-kitchen renting enterprise. This would grow into a sizeable business and soon it was taking up most of her time.

Walter had two sisters – both now dead – Sadie and Unity who was given a name, unusual to the streets of Glasgow, as a tribute to an English granny. In his formative years he saw too little of his mother. And his father Archie, who was a commercial traveller, was away from home for long periods representing his confectionery firm, Todd, Cunningham and Petrie, around shops in Troon, Largs and the Firth of Clyde holiday resorts. Perhaps something of Archie's genes surfaced in Walter's great passion for natty dressing – an obsession that has remained with him all his long life. Archie was extremely well spoken and well dressed – indeed, his mates nicknamed him Lord Nuffield as a comment on his style.

There was some childhood bonding when Archie, who gave up his Catholic religion on marriage, used to take wee Walter on what were called brake outings – nowadays we would just call them football supporters' away trips – to watch his beloved Celtic play away from home in places like Dundee. Often, on these outings, the wee fella was taken into pubs and clubs and seated on top of a piano, ready to bring a tear to the eye with a rendition of a song remembering the tragic death of Celtic keeper John Thomson in an Old Firm match. After Walter's warbling rendition, a collection was taken. Thomson was known as 'The Prince of Goalkeepers' and the accident happened in September 1931. Walter can still sing the words to this day:

A young lad named John Thomson,
From the west of Fife he came,
To play for Glasgow Celtic and
To build himself a name.
On the fifth day of September,
'Gainst the Rangers club he played.
He saved the Celtic from defeat,
Ah, but what a price he paid.

The ball rolled to Sam English,
And John ran out and dived.

The ball rolled on but John lay still,
For a hero he had died.

I took a trip to Parkhead,
To the dear old Paradise,
And, as the players made their appearance,
Sure a tear fell from my eye.
For a famous face was missing,
From the green and white parade,
And they told me Johnny Thomson,
In his last game he had played.

So play up Glasgow Celtic –
Stand up and play the game –
For, between your sticks, a spirit stands –
Johnny Thomson is his name.

Other than the outings to watch Celtic, Walter tells of primary school days that were spent looking after himself and, as we shall see, his criminal exploits largely denied him any secondary schooling at all. Father Archie was away at the commercial travelling and his mother would be out, night after night, looking after her room rentals and anything else that went with it. He was given six old pence a day and left to his own devices. But he did have a routine to spending his money. One penny went on a pie and gravy for lunch and another one was spent on a pudding. Then, at teatime, half of the four pence left went on a twopence 'dodger' from a fish and chip shop in Corn Street. A dodger was a half portion of fish and a few chips. The remaining twopence went on a night at the 'Wee Phoenix' – the sort of fleapit cinema that Glaswegians liked to describe as a place you itched to get in to and scratched to get out of – a penny to get in and a last penny for sweets.

Walter has a close and complex relationship with his daughter

Rita, a remarkable character in her own right. And she observes that, while such a regime might satisfy the inner man's hunger, something more important was mostly missing – love and companionship. The time Walter spent at the Wee Phoenix will perhaps touch a chord with the censorship lobby. Walter was certainly influenced by the films he regularly watched from such a young age.

At the Phoenix, he saw a film about John Dillinger, the legendary American gangster who specialised in armed robbery and terrorised Indiana and the neighbouring states in the early thirties. The movie may have given Walter the urge to be a gangland boss but, even at his tender age, he was still critical of the US gangster. Walter, as a youngster, believed he could have run the Dillinger mob and organised his heists better than the Yank. And maybe history has proved that wee Glasgow boy was right – after all, John Herbert Dillinger was gunned down in the streets of Chicago by the FBI at the early age of thirty-one. In his eighties, Walter Norval still struts the Glasgow stage and no one takes liberties with him to this day. Incidentally, Dillinger was a pretty sharp dresser, too – pinstripes and guns seem to have some kind of natural affinity.

But Walter Norval's early forays into crime had little Hollywood glamour about them. Almost the first things he stole were potatoes from the barrels which stood outside fruit and vegetable shops. The loot from such robberies was delicious when cooked over a bonfire in a tenement back court and shared with other urchins who were running around the streets.

However, an early minor criminal escapade was to have all the hallmarks of the quick thinking and planning that were to become the Norval trademark. Indeed, what the management consultants of today would call 'forward planning' was a Norval must – so much so that, in later life, when Glasgow's hard-nosed detectives encountered a particularly well-organised piece of thievery, the finger of suspicion almost automatically pointed to him. As a youngster of eight, the quick thinking lad's need to get his hands on cash was evident but there was a little less thought given to what would happen after the scam was over. Actually, and surprisingly, it started with an attempt to take up gainful employment – something that was not be a major feature in Walter Norval's long life of crime.

In the thirties, long before smokeless fuel and the awareness that hundreds of tenement fires, fuelled with coal, were causing smogs and deaths in the cold damp Glasgow winters, the streets were busy, on a daily basis, with coalmen hawking their wares which included what were called briquettes – slabs of compressed coal dust. A bit cheaper than the actual coal, briquettes produced a thick choking, yellowish smoke that was most unpleasant to breathe and which, undoubtedly, constituted a severe health hazard. Along with a young pal, Walter took to helping the local briquette man by running up and down the stairs with deliveries. It wasn't as hard work as that of the coalmen themselves, carrying huge rough and dirty sacks of fuel on their backs and climbing stairs like pack animals, but, nonetheless, it was tiring and dirty work.

One night, about six in the evening, Walter and his young friend were in Partick, some way from where they stayed on the Garscube Road, when enough seemed to have become enough and they demanded their wages so they could go home. The briquette man refused to pay. Walter thought out his next move. On the Saturday morning, he and his young pal were up at the crack of dawn and went round every house where they remembered the coalman had given coal or briquettes on tick, having agreed that the money would be collected on Saturday – provided the man of the house had not spent it at the bookies or in the pub on the Friday after collecting his weekly brown pay envelope. Walter and his pal went round the customers and collected quite a lot of cash by misrepresenting themselves as acting on behalf of the coalman. He had been slower out of his bed than the boys but he cottoned on to what had happened. After that, it was a number of weeks before the two young fraudsters could venture out on to the streets in safety. That was the first time Walter Norval went into hiding but it would not be the last.

Had the coalman found him, he would, no doubt, have given Walter a hiding and a warning about the error of his ways. But the warning would have fallen on deaf ears for, if there was one thing that was not in short supply in the childhood of Walter Norval, it was warnings that he would end up behind bars. But, in his youth, the long years of incarceration that lay ahead were never given a thought. Instead, his way of life, thieving where and when he could and amassing lots of ready cash that was spent freely on wee treats for his pals and generally playing the glad-hander, earned him the nickname 'Kid Millions'.

Walter was always a free spender and ready to share his ill-gotten gains with his associates – a trait that began almost from his first crime and has lasted through the dangerous years of armed robbery to today when many a pensioner in a local pub enjoys a free pint paid for out of a hefty roll of fivers. He tells of wandering into one local pub recently, looking around at the assembled geriatrics and buying everyone, except two healthy looking wannabe crims, a drink. When they asked why they were excluded from such generosity, the answer was simple enough. In Walter's view, they should be out 'tanning' a business or two and filling their wallets for themselves.

Right from the time when he was almost no bigger than a toddler, the local cops were on to him, warning of what would happen to him if he didn't mend his ways. When Walter looked out of his home in Garscube Road, above the Garscube Bar, he could look straight ahead at another famous pub of the era – Scott's. Garscube Road was known at the time as High Road and was not considered to be in Maryhill. It is hard to imagine these days, when most folk spend their nights glued to the telly, that, when Walter was growing up, there were around thirty pubs in the immediate area of his house. He can remember the names and locations of most of them and he splits them into two groups. The most important ones, in his view, were the Glen Lyon, Fallon's, Round Toll Bar, Scott's, Duffy's, The Noggin, The Milestone and The Hairy Corner. The others were Griffins, Woodside Bar, The Peargrove, Ross's, O'Donald's, The Bear's Paw, MacParland's, Jack's Bar, Dirty Dick's, The Whangie, No Ones, McLeod's, The Thistle Bar, Star and Garter, The Firhill Bar, The Queen's Vaults, The Camp Bar, The Grove and Taylor's. Such an array of licensed premises meant there was plenty of work for the cops in the Northern Division and Friday and Saturday nights were always lively affairs.

Lyon Street was almost at the centre of all this action and, as a strategic site, it was deemed worthy of a police box – a black Tardis-like structure which played an important role in the days of foot patrols when Pandas were furry animals munching leaves in far off China, rather than patrol cars. Lyon Street was narrow, with rows of four-storey buildings, and about the length of two football pitches. Part of the street was waste ground where buildings had been pulled down. These pieces of open ground were used by the kids for football and, on Saturdays, there was a pitch-and-toss school which was strategically timed to fit in with the menfolk's collection of their wages and the distribution of dole money. Each close had four main landings and on each landing there were eight single-end flats and one shared toilet. It takes little imagination to understand why the social workers, in the days before the Second World War, called such places 'castles of misery'. In these conditions, it was common for children rarely to see blue sky or the moon and the stars.

But it would be wrong to go too far down that road – just as it is equally wrong to stare back into the past through rose-coloured spectacles. The truth lies somewhere in between. Walter remembers it as a street filled with good working-class people who shared what little they had. Everyone was not like him – always ready to steal or spill blood. When the weather was good the women sat in the back courts on stools. He remembers them breast-feeding their babies as he and his pals played around them. On these long summer afternoons, the husbands stood chatting at the corner of Garscube Road – for work could be hard to find – or outside the pub called The Hairy Corner at the other end of Lyon Street, near North Woodside Road.

And, when Walter was growing up, the main inhabitant of the Lyon Street police box was one of the real old school of Glasgow cops, a huge pipe-smoking Irishman called Dunky McSwan whom Walter can describe, with unfeigned affection more that sixty years later, as a good sort of old-fashioned cop. And he remembers that, from day one, McSwan had him down in his notebook as 'a bloody rascal' – a verdict that many would agree with years later. But, at the time, Dunky was fair game for any bit of fun the boys on the streets could think up.

Like all street cops of those days, a fair bit of the work involved going round, after dark, checking that premises were lockfast and Walter and his pals noticed one of Dunky's little idiosyncrasies. To save time, he didn't always shine his torch on the padlocks to see if all was well. Instead, he just tended to give them a pull to make sure they were locked. This suggested a ploy to the youngsters who got a cargo of dogs' dirt, smeared one of the locks with it and hid up a close to watch events. The lumbering Irishman checked the padlock in the usual way and then used his torch to confirm his worst fears. His shouts of 'Who put bloody dog keech here?' could be heard above the chatter and clink of glasses in the nearby pubs.

Another imaginative ploy to annoy Dunky involved the use of fish bones which were piled up under the edge of a door in premises likely to be inspected by Dunky. When he flashed his torch at the bottom of the door the luminosity of the fish bones reflected the light giving the impression that there was a light on in the shop. When not annoying the local constabulary, Walter and his tenement friends played games like 'hunch, cuddy, hunch' in which they hunkered on to the backs of each other, forming a sort of human chain that weaved around, trying to force one of the members of the chain to spill off.

Another favourite was a sort of hopping game in which the group hopped around, each on one leg, and tried to nudge each other onto the ground. Even that old favourite hide and seek had a special Garscube Road version called 'Blue Caur'. This referred to the trams that ran up and down beside the street kids' homes. The old Glasgow Corporation, aware that many potential customers could not read, let alone write, colour-coded the 'caurs' according to their routes. The blue tram trundled up the Garscube Road toward Maryhill and Lambhill and its frequency was used to measure the time you had to hide. The searcher would wait for the right tram to pass and shout, 'Blue caur – here I come!'

Street games apart, war was permanently declared between Dunky and Walter and his pals. The movements of the enemy, PC McSwan, were of great interest to Walter who knew to the second and nearest yard where the big beat polis would be. He timed him on his rounds and constantly kept an eye on his habits. This was important as the shops and businesses of the Garscube Road area were tempting to boys with a fancy to do a bit of opportunistic thieving.

Walter was also keenly aware that the rattling thunder of a tramcar on a cobbled street could be used to cover the sound of a brick breaking a plate glass window. And, in those far off days, street lighting was not the high power affair it is today. On a cloudy moonless night, the conditions were perfect for a smash and grab. The drill was to check that the polis were away on the their rounds, at the far end of the patch, wait for a tram to rumble past, in with the brick through the window and dive into the shop, looting anything of value, money in the till, eggs, milk, anything in short supply. The young thieves were back out on the street almost before the tram had passed. And they didn't even have to leg it too far. They just disappeared into the darkness of the nearest close and, for a couple of eggs, a mother, with a brood of weans and a hungry shipyard worker to feed, would hide a stash of stolen goods till the going was clear. Then the boys took it to the illegal street bookies, who were always able to buy for ready cash for themselves or their friends, or one of the spivs, who thrived on black marketeering, and you were in cash.

Best of all was to 'tan' a clothing shop where there was potentially a double whammy on offer – rolls of cloth AND clothing coupons that had been handed in for completed garments. Thompson's, a sweetie factory in the neighbourhood, was another favourite target. There you stole what you could, you ate as much as you were able to and sold the rest to kids – and parents – with a sweet tooth. Sweeties played a role in one of Dunky McSwan's losing battles with the Wee Mob, as Walter and his gang came to be known.

In those days, many shops had the bottom of the window barred with horizontal straps of wood, leaving only the remaining top third or so clear to let in some light. One such shop faced the old Lyon Street police box and so was under the nose of Dunky for most of the time. But the fact that the law was only yards away didn't deter the Wee Mob. One day, with Dunky out on his rounds, Walter and a friend broke in through the unprotected upper glass of the window and began to help themselves to boxes of sweets which they lobbed out on to the pavement. But, for once, the polis returned unexpectedly and Walter's partner in crime just had time to jump back out through the window and race down the street, pursued by the law. Walter hid in the shop and, undetected, watched as, later, the abandoned boxes of sweets made their way into the police box rather than back into the shop. A cynical Walter mused that maybe his old adversary, PC McSwan, had a particularly sweet tooth!

21

Walter Norval cannot claim he drifted into crime – he embraced it. From his earliest days, he was warned by family, friends, school-teachers and neighbourhood policemen that he was heading for trouble. The reality is that he was trouble from day one. Archie Norval, Walter's father, had delivered his share of warnings to his wayward son but he died suddenly just as Walter was entering his teens – a particularly crucial age for a youngster to lose a parent and especially for a boy to lose his dad. The loss of his father's influence was compounded by his mother's long absences from home while she saw to her room-letting business and so it was that Walter was left without any real discipline.

But it was not a childhood completely filled with petty thieving. Fighting and fighting men played a major role in Walter's early life. Bloody bare fist battles on Sunday afternoons were regularly held on rough ground on the banks of the Forth and Clyde canal in these days.

Many of these fights came out of disputes that began in the host of pubs in the area. Rather than wreck the bar and everyone else's night out, there was often an agreement to settle an argument or perceived slur with a 'square jig' on the Sunday afternoon. Men fought, stripped to the waist, with bare fists and little respect for the rules of the Marquis of Queensberry. There were no three minute rounds or time limits and no pre-fight medicals or doctors or ambulances on hand. This was red, raw and blood-stained. Fights went on till one opponent submitted. Crowds of thirty or more watched and acted as some sort of referee with regard to low blows. The local police paid little or no attention. Presumably the thought of local hard men knocking lumps out of each other was not a prime concern. Better blood spilled on the canal banks than on the streets. Head butting was allowed, if the flying fists of your opponent let you near enough to inflict a 'Glasgow kiss', but blows below the belt were not on.

Aged around six or seven, Walter would steal up to the canal bank to watch these fights, usually shinning up a telegraph poll to reach the iron rungs that allowed you to climb even higher to get the best view of the brutal events. Such a hobby no doubt helped breed an ongoing respect and admiration for bare-fist, bare-chest battling. Walter Norval ended up as one of the most prolific armed robbers in Britain and no one knew better than him how to use weapons as the ultimate enforcer in old Wild West style or in Mafia fashion.

But his own fearsome fists brought respect, too. Quite naturally, with his background, he has always had an interest in legitimate boxing and he also has a remarkable memory of fights and fighters. One famous amateur, whose career he followed, was Dick McTaggart who won Olympic gold in Melbourne in 1956. For a spell, Dick was well known to Glasgow folk as he went about the city streets plying his trade as a rat catcher. Walter remembers that this decent man won the award as the outstanding stylist at the Aussie Games. McTaggart, who was perhaps the greatest amateur boxer never to turn pro, would, in later life, enjoy a pint or two in the Garscube Road pubs favoured by Walter and his connections. Fighting did seem to be a family interest.

As a kid going home after an exciting afternoon as a spectator on the canal bank, he would regale his ma, if she was around, with the tales of the fights and she would ask, with unfeigned interest, who had won, just as if they were talking about some million dollar battle arranged by Don King for Madison Square Garden and satellite TV.

Some of these open-air fights involved local street fighters and men who went on to make a career in the legitimate world of the square ring. One famous bout was between John 'The Bull' McCormack and a battler known as Hugh Keverner. McCormack also fought Willie Whyte who went on to defeat Jake Kilrain, one of Glasgow's best known pro-boxers, in a title bout. Whyte also won an award for bravery after he pulled a survivor from a burning plane. No one who survived the High Road or the Twilight Zone in the thirties and forties was without guts.

Two well-known Garscube Road characters, John Foy of Caithness Street and Joe O'Hara of Lyon Street, were involved in such open-air wars – wars that won the combatants respect equal to that accorded to the likes of Mike Tyson. Joe O'Hara's best remembered opponent was Mouse Drummond and John Foy had a memorable bout with Basher Owens.

Once the fights in the High Road were over, the matter often ended, despite the bloody nature of the battle, in a handshake. And that was it till the next drunken night, the next feud that had to be settled by a 'square jig'. Surprisingly, Walter recalls that there was little betting on the results – the sight of two strong men, battling each other to the point of exhaustion or perhaps to near death, with bare fists, was excitement enough. Fights generally took place at an area called the 'piggy'. This was up behind the Round Toll, the major intersection at the end of the Garscube Road where the roads led north, deeper into Maryhill, in the west, and south towards the villas of Great Western Road. In the days of Walter and the Wee Mob, a policeman stood directing traffic from a platform in the middle of the junction. Today it is an ugly, featureless conglomeration of traffic lights and road signs.

Glasgow in the thirties had a number of small urban farms that had survived the building of the tenements, small plots of ground where a pig or two could rut in the mud or where there was enough grass to keep a few cows or geese. Hence the waste ground known as the 'piggy'. Garscube Road, of course, adjoins the Cowcaddens, a city centre area with a name that harks back to its days of agriculture. Indeed, it was to lush grazing land in these parts that the early dairymen, who used Glasgow Green, would drive their cattle up Cow Loan (now Queen Street) to the lands at the top of Buchanan Street. These dairymen operated an early form of collective on the banks of the Clyde with the ownership of the beasts shared. But the 'piggy' was a far cry from the lush pasture lands that drew the cows on the trek up the hill from the Green.

The Forth and Clyde canal itself runs along the top of Maryhill, almost to the centre of town, with Port Dundas a few miles away. This area now, between the city's ring road and canal, is a gloomy mixture of car salerooms, warehouses and cash and carries – dreary and oppressive. But, when the canal first opened up the area in 1790, it was a state-of-the-art industrial development with the waterway providing a transport infrastructure for what we would now call a thriving industrial estate. There, brewing, dying, chemical manufacture and sugar refining were all going full blast.

But the chemical works left an unwanted heritage for Pinkston and Sighthill – the 'stinky ocean'. This was an area of damp ground where the chemicals had, down the years, permeated into the depths of the soil, emitting distinctive and unpleasant odours. The smell or the very real danger of infection did nothing to deter the ragged barefoot children of the thirties who found the 'stinky ocean' a place of attraction – an adventure playground more exciting by far than a modern swing park or skateboard arena provided by a benevolent council. Today the area has largely been built on but there are plenty of folk to tell you that the pong of the 'stinky ocean' can still occasionally be sniffed in the air. Apart from the 'ocean' and the nearby 'piggy', another venue for open-air grudge battles was the Braid's Brae.

The canal bank was home to more than fighting. Pitch-and-toss was massively popular in the thirties and drew huge crowds of gambling men to the canal bank. Hard men were in demand as 'belt men' to guard the cash pile. A whack over the head with fast-swinging, brass-buckled, heavy leather belt was not something that you took lightly. Pitch-and-toss schools had rules that were every bit as rigorous as any Las Vegas blackjack table. Coins were placed on a stick and tossed high in the air and punters wagered large sums on the chance of two heads or two tails landing together in the mud of the canal tow path. The spectacle and the chance of a big win could attract hundreds. Such a place and such a life was a fertile breeding ground for hard men. And Walter Norval was to become the hardest of the hard. But, before that, there were to be many youthful criminal adventures ahead for the King of the Twilight Zone.

2

REALITY AND
ROSE-COLOURED SPECTACLES

There are two schools of thought about life up a close in the Glasgow of yesteryear – and two sorts of closes. There were the douce, so-called 'wally closes' which had, and still have in many areas of the city, nicely tiled walls and doors with art nouveau or art deco stained-glass inserts. Such closes lead up, via carefully white-washed stairs, to homes with polished brasses and gleaming dark-brown furniture. Such little palaces of tenement life are mostly to be found in middle-class areas like Dennistoun and the West End. In areas like Maryhill and the Gorbals, where money and gainful employment were clearly in much shorter supply, the tenement homes might still have the highly polished range and might be just as well kept but it was often a struggle to survive.

The shelves of Glasgow's many libraries creak from the weight of books galore that paint a picture of a cosy life, even in the Gorbals – sometimes especially in the Gorbals – seen though rose-coloured spectacles. In this fantasy world, the neighbours all helped each other and the struggle against a fate that had condemned them to such a slum was fought with a communal intensity and cheerfulness. In this version of tenement life, the self-help of folk thrown together breeds the kind of congeniality and community spirit and values you couldn't buy.

This rose-coloured version concentrates on some of the

undoubted positive aspects of life in a tenement but ignores the downside of outside toilets, muddy and unhygienic back-courts and drunken noisy neighbours. The rose-coloured view of tenement life makes much of the success of lawyers, doctors and men of science who hauled themselves out of the pit of adversity and went on to change the world. And, indeed, there are some spectacular examples of this happening. In the twenty first century, as the true reality seeps away into distant memory and many of the old tenements themselves fall to the wrecker's ball, the rosy hue of this vision seems to grow stronger by the year. A cynic might get the impression that, at times, life up a close even in the toughest of Glasgow areas was more desirable than the life in the garden suburbs that the folk, who actually lived the tenement life, dreamed of.

Other writers have wallowed in tales of squalor and crime – drawing attention to the effects on the health of children, who were brought up in damp, under-heated homes without baths or showers, and highlighting the difficulty of doing homework and other hardships in a crowded single end. And they, too, have examples to prove their case – the stories of men nailed to wooden floors by thugs and razor wielding neds strutting the streets and sending a chill of fear into all who crossed their paths. And the cell blocks of Barlinnie were, at any given time, filled with gangsters born and bred up a close in a slum.

For years, there have been streets that are no-go areas to those not prepared to defend themselves with their fists, a blade or, in extreme cases, a firearm. And most of Glasgow's gangsters emerged from tenement life – even if later their ill-gotten gains let them move to villas and bungalows where they hid the source of their wealth from neighbours, wearing Armani suits, driving heavily chromed and highly polished 4x4s and masquerading as 'businessmen' by day and villains by night.

The truth is that, of course, life up a close was a mixture of both viewpoints. There was community. There was fun. There was squalor. There was crime. The early years of a violent Godfather like Walter Norval give testimony to that. And the story of his formative years is speckled with every aspect of tenement life – from the conviviality to the violence. And it is hard to underestimate the effect a tenement upbringing had on the man he became. Almost from day one, he built up an admiration for the hard men of the area. Barely out of short trousers, he was developing a conscienceless approach to life – a philosophy that said, if you need it, take it.

In those far off days, in the dark back-courts of the High Road, might was seen as right and admiration was doled out to those tough enough to survive and prosper in the hardest of hard schools. The High Road was generally considered to be the area from the corner of New City Road and Stewart Street up to the Round Toll and it was here that a Glasgow Godfather was to be moulded. It was a place far removed from the High Street around Glasgow Cross – the first home of Glasgow's ancient and much respected university. There was a rich amalgam of pubs, fish and chip shops, dance halls, a picture house, grocers', bakers' and fruit and vegetable shops. And, of course, in Tower Buildings, there was a snooker hall that was much favoured by wannabe gangsters and their pals.

The old saying that ability with a snooker cue reflected a wasted life was not a million miles from reality. Many a robbery was planned as the reds and blacks spun into the pockets with a speed brought on by much practice – a speed that would have impressed Hurricane Higgins himself. Many large 'coarse notes', as that legendary chronicler of New York's gangsters Damon Runyon called dollar bills with high face values, changed hands over a frame or two. Within this tight little area, there was all that was necessary for a city centre 'village'. Glasgow had many such places but the High Road was special with its own brand of rough community.

An illustration of this is told with relish by Walter Norval.

His massive capacity for thieving and fighting and generally creating mischief meant that, from his days in short trousers up to his first spells behind bars, he was always wary of a blue uniform. And, indeed, from the days of Dunky McSwan onwards, Glasgow's finest kept an eagle eye open for Norval's movements. If he seemed to be missing, there was sure to be trouble around somewhere. But that legendary spirit of community meant that this Godfather-in-waiting could rely on his neighbours to side with him rather than with the law.

In the days in the top flat at 291 Garscube Road, he seldom left the house without a quick peek out of the top floor window. Across the street, the women, gossiping and passing the time of day in their various close mouths, would glance up and down the road for any lurking boys in blue before giving the rogue the all clear to leave the nest. That was the kind of solidarity that typified tenement life in the High Road.

Walter's most formative days were spent in that flat. Scott's bar was just across the main road and Duffy's pub and the Milestone were on the same side of the street as Norval's close. Just a few yards away, were two of the most famous closes in the area, one of which was home to the legendary street bookie Laurie Venters. The fun of life up a close could be rough-edged in its humour and Walter tells a classic incident much remembered in the area.

Drink, not surprisingly considering the number of pubs and wine shops in the area, played a major role as the fuse that ignited trouble on the streets or acted as a lubricant when villainy was in the planning stage. But sometimes there were occasions when the drink and its effects had their amusing side. Ginger McVey is remembered by Walter as a man who was handy as a babysitter for a wife who liked to go out to the Wee Phoenix picture house of an evening. In the Glasgow patois, 'ginger' means lemonade or it can be applied more widely to refer to any soft drink. It would seem that it was his hair colour that gave

30

Ginger his nickname rather than a liking for soft drinks. For Mr McVey, as a regular reward for his selfless provision of babysitting services, got two large jugs of cheap strong red wine a night for his sole consumption.

Incidentally, in Glasgow wine shops, right up until the fifties, you could still see old and bent wives, wrapped in their shawls, taking their jugs to be filled with the cheap red 'biddy'. A glass or ten of this stuff may have been harmful to the liver but it did smooth out some of the rough edges of life in the slums. Shops like Oddbins and Haddows, now such a familiar sight on the city streets, and wines from Australia, Argentina, and Chile were a distant dream in these days.

One night, Garscube Road and the streets around it were suddenly alive with uniformed police and detectives. A distraught mother had declared one of her children missing. The cops were deployed in force for a major hunt for the missing child. This was serious stuff. Stair-heid rammies were regular occurrences – as were street-corner battles between the odd drunk or, indeed, a couple of youthful gangs. The police going about their business, sorting out such routine events, were a familiar sight. But this was different.

The tenement folk love their weans. And this night there was a nasty feeling on the streets. A toddler was missing – perhaps abducted or even murdered. For a time, it looked a black scenario and the close-knit community feared the worst. The hunt went on for hours, from close to close, with tearful mothers wondering what on earth had happened. But, for once, there was a happy ending – the missing wean had been safely tucked up in bed by Ginger the babysitter. The child had popped in to play with Ginger's young charges and, when it was time for bed, our befuddled hero, who had made a major early assault on his two jugs of red biddy, simply swept them up and tucked all in sundry into bed, neglecting even to count the weans in his charge – a task that, in any case, would have been beyond him at that time of night. And then he had fallen into the deep sleep of the just, oblivious to the distress and drama he had caused.

An abiding memory of the folk who lived in tenements is of the importance of the back street bookie in the order of things. These were hard times with cash and jobs difficult to find and, sometimes, food, too, was in short supply. The illegal street bookies sold dreams. A winning line could make a world of difference to the folk who stood around street corners with time on their hands, reading the racing pages in between taking a look at the few advertised jobs on offer. This was a world far removed from today's high street betting shops, with arty photographs of the classic races in the window and centrally-heated, brightly lit interiors, to draw the gamblers in out of the cold and rain of the street.

Illegal bookies took 'lines' from the punters in all weathers and lookouts would be posted to warn of the approach of cops. The punters used noms de plume and the very illegality of the operation added a little extra excitement to the betting itself. The bookie's runner was a substitute occupation for hundreds of unemployed men who took the cash and bets of the gainfully employed and relayed them to the bookies themselves. There was, however, some similarity to today in that, most of the time, the cash went into the bookies' sacks, never to return to the ever-optimistic punters.

The Garscube Road area was a hotbed of such illegal gambling and the lines were just a way of life for the men. Names like Laurie Venters became almost legendary as bookies. Near the close where Venters lived was the home of another character who loomed large in those formative years for Norval – one Biadge Jaconelli, conveniently know to all and sundry as 'B'. Jaconelli made a speciality of collecting the lines from the Italians who ran the hundreds of fish and chip shops and ice-cream parlours, that were a way of life in Glasgow, and laid them off with bookies like Venters. Though, if 'B' liked the look of bet, he often held the cash himself in his own book.

'B' was big bull of a man, well able to look after himself in a tough area. He had been brought to Scotland aged a mere ten months and, of course, during the war and afterwards his citizenship status was questionable. He was, in fact, deported back to Italy for eighteen months after he had punched a youth in some dispute or other. He made a fine job of it, too, sending the lad backwards through a shop window. Life wasn't easy for 'B' back in Italy since he could not speak a word of Italian. Eventually, on his return home, after the authorities had relented over his status as a Scot, he told Walter of long days on a relative's farm mumbling in a thick Glasgow accent to the sheep that flocked on the sunny hillside.

Jaconelli was just one of a remarkable collection of Garscube Road characters. Dots Docherty was another well remembered by Walter Norval. Docherty was what Glaswegians call 'a modeller', a term indicating that the person concerned lived in one of the city's many 'model' lodging houses which had been built to provide cheap, basic living quarters for itinerant labourers and such but which also attracted their fair share of down-and-outs and alcoholics.

Docherty had more than one hundred convictions for breach of the peace and was always shouting and bawling at close-mouths. In particular, he subjected the bookies, Venters and Jaconelli, to his unwanted attentions – despite the fact that the bookies didn't just tolerate him but were actually kind to him on many occasions. Inevitably, the police would lift him and take him down the road to Maitland Street, the Northern Police Office, and, on Monday, he would either be fined or jailed for thirty days. If he was lucky enough to be fined, either Venters or Jaconelli paid it for him.

Maggie Purdon was another character on the Garscube Road. She was a lookout for the street bookies despite suffering the handicap, in such a job, of having only one eye. This, on one occasion, led to a policeman slipping by on her blind side but, before he could reach the bookie in the back court, Maggie realised her mistake, ran down the close, jumped on the copper's back and so gave the bookie time to escape. In the evenings Maggie went to the window of her flat, almost directly across the road from Walter's, and played a selection of tunes on her saxophone. Walter liked to stand at the window and listen to the sweet emotive melodies floating on the summer air. And often he was rewarded with a friendly wave from this remarkable character – a poignant memory from a way of life now gone.

The Jaconelli home played a large part in Walter's early life. Little happened in his own home during the day and his mother Eva often took him round to the Jaconelli room and kitchen where the future hard man of the streets and prisons spent hours playing with the Jaconelli daughter Angie. Walter and Angie virtually grew up together and there was one of those sort of family understandings/beliefs, on both sides, that, one day, they would marry. In any event, they were often tucked up in bed together – but only at the tender age of three or so when Tizzy (Mrs Jaconelli) and Eva went out at night to hen parties.

As they grew older, Walter and Angie stayed close but in a brotherly and sisterly sort of way. The expected marriage never took place but, more than fifty years later, Walter still talks about Angie and her family with genuine affection. With the Jaconellis, he found something of the warmth and family that, for long periods, seemed to be missing in his own home. And maybe he enjoyed the simple companionship while his mother Eva spent long spells working as a waitress down the Ayrshire coast during the summer holidays or was fully occupied with looking after her flats. It may have been fun for the holidaymakers enjoying cheap and cheerful beach breaks but it was part of an often lonely childhood that shaped Walter Norval's life. The Jaconellis were just a couple of closes away but Walter remembers it as a

34

happy world. His 'romance' with young Angie was just the start of a spectacular career as a ladies' man for Walter.

Another local character of those days, Pop McCausland, has stayed long in the Norval memory. At the McCausland fireside, he listened, with rapt attention, to tales of the old days in Ireland – from where many thousands of the inhabitants of Glasgow's tenements originally had come seeking work. Stories of rural life in a far off and green land and tales of women reputed to be witches and men of great strength were told over the flickering fireside flames. And they made a great impression on young Norval. Later in life, when he was deep in trouble, Pop McCausland would re-emerge to play an important role in Walter's life of crime.

Memory plays funny tricks and, looking back at your childhood, some incidents and places seem to stand out. Those days at the McCausland's and the Jaconelli's were happy highlights in a childhood full of black patches and dark deeds. Even the geography of our childhood haunts can have its effect on memory. One of the most potent memories for the now elderly denizens of the High Road is of the area's famous 'teapot close'. Unlike its neighbours, this close was named after a shop rather than taking the name of the most dominant family who lived up it. In the old days, house numbers were not all that important and a close was usually known as Buchanan's or McKay's or whatever. The 'teapot close' was, therefore, some-thing special.

Glasgow of the thirties and forties was well served by local grocers' shops. The grocers' chains then were not multi-nationals but famous Scottish names like Lipton's, Cooper's, Massey's and Cochrane's. Fresh butter was sold by the pat, there would be a selection of teas extensive enough to baffle a connoisseur and, above all, the shop had an unforgettable rich and warm smell of cake, bread and fresh food generally. Virtually nothing was pre-wrapped and the provisions were handed over in brown paper pokes that had their own distinctive smell. Usually the name above the door was in huge highly polished brass letters. But the branch of Cochrane's in the Garscube Road had an eye-catching trademark. The shop had a large golden coloured replica of a teapot hanging outside and, of course, the close beside it was christened the 'teapot close'. The golden teapot itself was like a lighthouse to help those in need to navigate the area.

Such friendly shops were generally thrown out of business by the arrival of cash-and-carry grocery chains and multi-nationals, like Safeway, but they are remembered with genuine affection by the folk who used them. However, man does not live by bread alone, as they say, and equally well remembered are the bookies, the vendors of dreams. Maybe even some of cash from a winning line would be spent at Cochrane's on a wee treat for the family. But it is odds on that most of a win would end up in the till of bars like The Bear's Paw or The Tam O'Shanter, an establishment that was also handy for the Corn Street fish and chip shop.

Any successful bookie has access to large sums of ready cash and Laurie Venters could take occasional notions to spread it around in some style, buying punters drinks with the money he had won from them. However, some of his cash surplus was put to more worthwhile use. In his heyday, he operated from an 'office' up a close where much of the paperwork, such as it was, was handled. Many of the residents of the close had their rents looked after for them by the bookie. The actual placing of lines was done in back-courts and other shady areas away from the prying eyes of the cops. But, like many a street bookie, Venters had friends in blue uniforms who turned a blind eye to the illegal gambling or tipped him off about raids.

And he was always ready for the occasional over-zealous cop trying his hand at a surprise raid. The bookie would assemble half a dozen or so fake punters who were paid a pound as a fee to be caught illegally betting. These characters, who were happy to be of service – there was often something of a waiting list for the bookie's pound – were taken to the Northern Police Station and fined but the fines would come out of the bookie's satchel. Venters had the routine down to a fine art and he always took trouble even to hold fake lines for the guys who were to be caught. Care was taken to make sure genuine bets were recorded and honoured.

The cornerstone of the whole system was, of course, the nom de plume. Walter Norval, who, to this day, spends an inordinate amount of time in betting shops, didn't show much imagination in his choice of nom de plume in these far off gambling days. Even then, his name carried some weight and his initials, WN, were deemed OK for his betting slip nom de plume. Other punters chose more anonymous tags.

Laurie Venters used to pay out on a Saturday night and there was an element of trust here as it was impossible to put a face to every nom de plume and this led to some amusing Runyon-esqe incidents. One of Venters' regulars was a character called Wee Joe Ramsay who, on one occasion, missed out on a winning bet because he didn't have a copy of the pay-out sheet that recorded the wagers, the winners and their winnings. But he took a sneaky look over another punter's shoulder and saw that the nom de plume Mac 291 had £5 15s noted against it as yet to be collected. He then strolled out of the back-court across the road to the Milestone pub where he bought a friendly Irishman a pint and asked him if he'd do him a little favour. Would his new friend oblige him by nipping over to the bookie's to pick up his winnings? The amount, he told him, was more than a fiver – a tidy sum in these days. So off the Irishman went and presented himself as Mac 291 and collected the cash. Back in the Milestone, Wee Joe and his pal celebrated in style. But, of course, when the real Mac 291 turned up to claim his winnings from the bookie, the cash had gone. Venters smelled a rat and made for the Milestone where he met the Irishman, though by now Wee Joe was long gone. 'Who put you up to this?' demanded the bookie.

'A wee man,' replied the Irishman.

'What sort of wee man?' asked Venters.

The pub collapsed in laughter when he was given the answer, 'A really dacent wee man!'

Some of the street bookies, like Venters enjoyed their cat-and-mouse existence with the law and, since they operated without official premises, they needed the support of their punters and their neighbours. Laurie Venters had a reputation for treating his neighbours well and it worked in his favour. Apart from paying the odd rent demand, he was also said to be something of a soft touch when a loan was required to put mince on the table till the weekly pay packet arrived. This was not, however, the sort of illegal money-lending that became so prevalent in the slums later on when loan sharks charged high interest and both your financial and physical health were endangered if you didn't pay it back. Nor was there any question of acquiring giros and unemployment money from folk with a drug problem as is the modern moneylender's way. This was a fiver here, a tenner there, passed out in the knowledge that it would be repaid in due course.

In those bad old days, there were plenty of folk who needed a helping hand with the folding stuff from time to time. And, for a street bookie operating from his room and kitchen and without formal backup staff, it was handy indeed that the neighbours didn't take exception either to the hordes who climbed the stairs to seek him out or to the fact that he used his home as an office. And, of course, in wartime and after, with food and other goods rationed, the bookie was in a good position to act as a fence for the proceeds of the countless petty robberies that took place – they had both the cash and the contacts for this.

So, although there was some sense of community and fun to be had from life in a tenement close in a hard-necked area, it would be a serious mistake to allow this to obscure the underlying misery of substandard housing, overcrowding and poverty. And you can't underestimate the effect this kind of upbringing had on shaping of the criminal life of Walter Norval and his fellow villains who were brought up in similar conditions in the Gorbals and the East End of Glasgow and who took to violence and thieving in a big way. Rose-coloured spectacles are not appropriate.

3

RUMBLE ON THE LOCHSIDE

Glaswegians like to remark that you can take the boy out of Glasgow but you can't take Glasgow out of the boy. It can be a shrewd and accurate observation. The tale of Walter Norval's short, violent excursion into country life is a case in point. Walter's formative days were not spent entirely in the smoky tenement back-courts of Cowcaddens or on the muddy canal banks of Maryhill. There was a rural episode to his boyhood that was to end, as happened so often in his life, in trouble and a run-in with the police.

Lochgoilhead is an Argyll village and there the way of life is as different as any you could imagine from the overcrowding, noise and squalor of the old Garscube Road. To reach this tranquil rural retreat today you drive west out of Glasgow towards Helensburgh, on the banks of the Clyde. You then take one of the most beautiful drives in the world along the fabled west side of Loch Lomond and on up towards the summit of one of Scotland's most impressive mountain passes, the Rest and Be Thankful. Here, in the early days of motoring, drivers stopped and allowed their struggling, steaming engines to cool down after the effort involved in climbing up such a steep and winding hill. Over a coffee from a flask and a muttered thankfulness that the worst of the journey was over, the early tourists rested and were thankful that they had made it to the summit. They then climbed back into their cars and drove down the steep descent to the picturesque shores of Loch Fyne and the scenic, if dangerous, twisting road onwards either to Inveraray or Campbeltown.

The summit of the 'Rest' is still a fine place to stop and admire the view. It is one of the nicest picnic sites in the west of Scotland and there is the chance to enjoying a bacon buttie from the roadside stall that has been a favourite there for years. Turn sharp left at the summit, however, and you are on to a narrow, twisting road that leads down to sea level and the delights of Lochgoilhead – a quiet place where Glaswegians by the score have, for years, enjoyed a country break in a wee holiday cottage or a wooden cabin. The most excitement on offer is likely to be a fishing trip out on the loch, for a spot of mackerel-bashing, a walk round the impressive pile of Carrick Castle, overlooking the sea, or perhaps a slow, quiet pint with locals. Today, as it was in the twenties, thirties and early forties, Lochgoilhead is a slow-paced, sea-breezy sort of a place that offers immediate succour from the stresses of city life.

However, it has known moments of excitement – such as the time Walter Norval arrived. During the early days of the Second World War, Glasgow folk were all too aware of how the heavy industrial sites in the city and Clydeside generally could present prime targets for the Luftwaffe. They were fearful that mass air raids would decimate the civilian population. It was a fear that also gripped many parts of Britain. South of the border, young Londoners were packed on to trains and sent to quiet villages in Kent, surrounded by orchards, or to sprawling Devon farmhouses. Glaswegians mostly found themselves 'doon the watter' to the Firth of Clyde resorts or on campsites on Loch Lomondside. The Loch Lomondside option was not as safe as it seemed since German bombers often took to dropping, at random, any unused bombs, from raids on the shipyards, just a few miles over the hills at Clydebank, over the bonnie banks on the way home. It was even rumoured that many a pilot, afraid of the flak from anti-aircraft fire from the defensive positions

41

round the yards, simply dropped their bombs around the loch and hightailed it home to the Fatherland.

Evacuation of school-age children took place on a massive scale in these dark days. I found myself on a farm near John o'Groats where the geese seemed to take a delight in chasing me round the yard. To a six-year-old, the suburban south side of Glasgow seemed a far safer option than the countryside peopled with folk with odd accents and animals who seemed to offer an ever-present threat of injury and I was more than happy to return home.

For Walter Norval the blitz bolt-hole was Lochgoilhead where his mother had a little cottage. But the scenic drive over hill and around loch was not for him. He was packed on to a train to Gourock and taken round to the village by the *Comet*, one of the little steamers that plied round the firth, calling at places like Kilcreggan and Dunoon and taking people and cargo up the narrow fjord-like lochs that are such a major tourist attraction in the west of Scotland. The vessel's name was, of course, a tribute to James Watt's history-making steamer that once plied the same waters.

It must have been a beautiful sail – relaxing enough to calm the most turbulent soul, you might think. But his days there, surrounded by pine forest and sea rather than tenement, pub and bookie, didn't defuse the Norval fighting spirit. The 'vaccies', as the locals called the townies who had been evacuated, were already in the village in some numbers when he arrived. This was not appreciated by the local youngsters who, before Walter's arrival, were holding the upper hand and keeping the 'vaccies' under control in series of locals-versus-incomers rumbles.

No doubt the few fresh-faced local lassies were also a source of friction. And one young son of a local farm was considered by the 'vaccies' to be a particularly threatening bully. When Walter was told about him, he decided to step in as peacemaker. This, oddly, is a role he seems to have revelled in and playing it got him into some tough scrapes in his later days in prison when he would act with his trademark bloody violence to stop what he felt was unacceptable bullying. The method Walter chose on this occasion was the usual one of knocking the living daylights out of the bully. He was determined to show this bullying son of the soil that the 'vaccies' were people to be reckoned with. The delights of fresh air and farm eggs took second place to his mission to sort out this mini-war between two very different sorts of youngsters and he was soon wading in, fists flying, at the bully boy.

Not content with this show of force, his defiance and disregard for the forces of law and order were as dominant as they had been in the High Road and led to him having another rather different run-in with the law. While he was in the process of impressing all the youngsters of the area that might is right and that he had the might in the form of street-fighting skills honed in the big city, along came another couple of outsiders. These were two youngsters on the run from Mossbank Approved School. The school had been moved, en masse, from Ayrshire to Lochgoilhead to dodge the perceived threat of Nazi bombs – although, from this distance in time, one would have thought that rural Ayrshire was far enough away from the front line and hardly a prime target.

These two escapees chanced on Walter and, ever obliging, he allowed them to spend a couple of nights hiding out from the cops in his mother's wee cottage without her knowing a thing about it. But this was stretching even Walter's early organisational skills and, after a day or two, the lads surrendered to the police and were returned to the approved school.

Walter's talents as a leader were given an early test run in his sojourn in the hills and glens, far from the dark canyons of the tenements of Garscube Road and its environs. After he had 'tanned', as he puts it, the local bully, he started a little gang among the 'vaccies' giving the members nicknames like Romeo,

Soapy, Porky and the like. The locals had to take a back seat as this lot went on the rampage. They stole from the local shops, raided hen houses for the eggs, which were like gold in these days, and generally created mayhem in what had been a quiet backwater.

They had a gang hut, set into the mountainside, behind the village centre, and they used to go up to what they called the Rat Pit for bit of fun. The Rat Pit – in reality, the village dump for refuse – was a mile out of the village and, naturally enough, it was infested with rats. The gang went on frequent expeditions to kill the rats but were usually foiled. The city boys got an insight into animal life, however, as they noted that the rats seemed to be clever enough to post a 'sentry' in the long run to the centre of the pit. At the first sign of danger, this rat would race down the run, squealing a warning, and its fellow rodents would make their escape.

Another incident underlined that Walter was not cut out for country life. Sent to the local school, he became as big a problem there as he had been back in the city. One local lassie sat in front of him with her tempting golden pigtails hanging down over the back of her chair. The bold young Norval found the temptation to pull them too strong. In the ensuing rammy, Walter ran out of classroom with the teacher chasing after him. On the way out, Walter paused to lob a handy brick through the school window. That was it. The village policeman was summoned and thundered up to the school on his motorbike to collar the young villain.

He was sentenced to instant deportation from leafy Argyll and was sent back to the war-time darkness of the big city. So it turned out that he found himself back at sea on the *Comet*.

I doubt if he appreciated the glories of the scenery much. His father, angry at this predictable turn of events, was there to meet him. He was angry enough to give him a good cuffing and a severe dose of verbal abuse and he came to the unarguable conclusion that Walter was trouble wherever he was sent. An observation that was to be true for the next sixty years or so. This pier-head rammy between father and twelve-year-old son had a poignant touch as it was not long after this that Archie was to die of cancer. This meant he didn't have to suffer the infamy his errant son was to bring to the family name in the years to come but, equally, he didn't have the opportunity to try to steer him in the direction of a lawful life.

Despite the fact that the country idyll that went wrong was enough to enrage his old man so much, the experience failed to act as a warning and, like the others, it was ignored by a youngster who was seemingly destined to a life of crime. For Walter, there was no shame in being kicked out of Lochgoilhead. At this point, his days as an armed robber and gunman were still some years ahead but, if he had carried a gun in those days, there would have been another notch in it for Lochgoilhead – with his conscience as untroubled as ever.

However, his banishment had another curious effect that was to help mould him into a criminal. Back in Glasgow, there was confusion about what school he was at. Was he a pupil at Lochgoilhead or in city? He was registered at both but, of course, he was mostly playing pokey and, in reality, attended neither. This meant that, for long periods after primary school, he was never subject to the discipline or education on offer from a Scottish school system that, at the time, was the envy of Britain. And so another set of educational and character-building guiding hands was posted missing and the youngster left to his own trouble-making devices.

Whatever else he is or was, Walter Norval has a sharp brain – if little in the way of morality or scruples. Who knows what would have happened had he been exposed to his full quota of schooling. Perhaps if, instead of running with the rascals, he had had a teacher with the personality to inspire and be a role model, it would have made a difference – but I doubt it. The odds are that, even if he'd had the most inspiring teacher imaginable, the only difference that might have made would have been to turn him into a more literate gangster. All the signs are that his destiny had been decided almost from birth. The one thing Walter got praise for in his limited schooling was an ability to tell a tale. He had a way with words and an active imagination which, in later years, would help him out of many a tight scrape with the law.

Back on the streets, he now had a hero – and a plan. The hero was John Foy, the canal-side brawler, and the plan was to follow in Foy's footsteps to Polmont Borstal. This was not exactly the dream of a normally ambitious youngster but Walter's upbringing had set him apart. John Foy, together with his mate Joe O'Hara, formed a legendary hard man team. This infamous duo feature prominently in the newspaper archives of lowlife in Glasgow. In the forties and fifties, they were known as the 'Kings of the Garscube Road'. Foy, in particular, took a shine to young Walter and he watched his early thieving and the exploits of the Wee Mob, Norval's first gang, with interest. Indeed, it was John Foy who gave them their name and he followed their activities with almost fatherly pride.

One of the most dominant memories in the life of young Walter Norval was walking the streets of his patch in the company of John Foy. Foy had something Walter craved – respect. In the history of gangs and gangland, from the Mafia to the Chinese Tongs, from the Krays in the East End of London to the Thompsons in the East End of Glasgow, respect is a vital and hard-won commodity. As he strutted down the Garscube Road, everyone gave Foy the time of day, everyone showed respect for his powerful physique and reputation. John Foy was someone and, if you walked in his company, you were automatically someone too. More than sixty years later, during his daily visits to the betting shop or his strolls around the Round Toll and what is left of his old haunts, Walter Norval commands something of the same respect.

In his young mind, Walter equated some of the respect given to Foy to the fact that Foy had been incarcerated in Scotland's most infamous borstal at Polmont, near Falkirk, in Scotland's central belt. Borstal establishments were sort of halfway houses between approved schools and big-time prisons like Peterhead, Perth or Barlinnie. As a youth custody scheme, it was fundamentally flawed and, when Walter was finally sentenced to a spell there, he had firsthand experience of both the brutality and the complete failure to rehabilitate the youngsters sentenced to be caged in such a grim place. What was even worse was the fact that Walter Norval left borstal not only with no desire to go straight but with the feeling that he had graduated with first class honours from the university of crime.

All that was in the future – the here and now was strutting along the Garscube Road in the company of its Kings and being seen as these hard men's young prince. Foy and O'Hara always had a number of ploys on the go at any one time. One of them was to run a lucrative pitch-and-toss school at Sighthill and this, of course, gave Walter an introduction to the gambling scene. But being under the wing of the Kings of the Garscube Road, though undoubtedly exciting, also involved some more mundane duties.

Walter remembers running for John Foy's meals during the Sunday gambling schools. As the stakes piled high and the 'beltman' guarded the piles of cash, Walter would run to Foy's mother-in-law's house, in Glenmavis Street, Cowcaddens, for plates of cabbage, tatties and ham and ferried them back up to the gamblers. Walter ran all sorts of errands for Foy and was paid £1 after school to be at the big man's beck and call. This was a considerable sum in those days, indeed many a man earned not much more for a week's legitimate toil. Such cash helped contribute to the Norval nickname 'Kid Millions' that he wore with pride around the High Road.

The pitch-and-toss school had originally been run by a local character called Haggerty but Foy, O'Hara, a professional boxer called Willie Whyte, a couple of hard men called Joe Kerr and Big Jim Toner and a few others simply walked in one day and, by force of their fists, took control of this nice little earner. From then on, Walter was up with the gamblers every Sunday, hanging about on the outside of the circle, kicking a ball about with his friends and waiting to see what John Foy wanted him to do. Every once in a while, a policeman would turn up and the gamblers would turn around to watch Walter and the Wee Mob playing football as if that was all that was going on and was the only reason for such a crowd to be in such a place on a Sunday.

When the law went away, satisfied that every thing was hunky-dory and above board, the gambling would resume. Walter would then trouser a pound and his boys would get five bob each for their trouble. Walter used to lie to Foy and exaggerate the number of lads he had engaged for this ploy – keeping the extra cash himself, of course. Foy was wont to remark, 'Walter, you're conning me!' And young Norval would keep a straight face and reply, 'Honest, John, there was eight or nine up – some are away home for their dinners.' The big-time gambler got a laugh out of this piece of enterprising cheek and promised that, one Sunday, he would count the footballers. But the fifteen-year-old Norval was trusted by Foy to run his messages and there was genuine affection between them. Sixty years on, Walter says, 'He trusted me and treated me like a little brother which he never had. I felt he was the big brother I had lost as a child.'

The memories flood back. On Victory in Europe night in May 1945, folk of Garscube Road and the surrounding streets lit bonfires. While they sang and danced, Walter and his friends Biggy and Harris were busy on other matters – forcing open a safe in a contractor's yard and stealing £40. They then went back to the bonfires to join the girls and, now in funds, treat them to fish and chips. And around this time, Foy and O'Hara got themselves jailed for fighting at the Tower Ballroom door. That night, John's wife got Walter to take fish and chips and lemonade to the Northern Police Office where her husband was held. The officer on duty fell for Walter's ready chat and allowed the food in. The bold youngster told the officer that Foy and O'Hara hadn't been able to get anything to eat because they had been arrested at their work.

The battling at the ballroom door became a regular occurrence and the Kings of the Garscube Road were arrested for fighting time after time. But they were not the only hard men. Walter tells of meeting a 'fighting man' who was well known and said to rule 'the town' as the Garscube Road folk called the city centre areas. This was Dan Cronin, a legendary old-time Glasgow crime figure, who had a reputation as a gunman and was certainly not a man to be messed around. Walter heard that Cronin was with Foy in the Noggin pub, facing the Milestone pub. Walter sought them out and told John Foy that he and his pals wanted to go to the pictures and hadn't any money. Cronin asked Foy who the boy was and was told, 'He's the leader of the Wee Mob and solid'. Cronin handed over half a crown – a lot in those days – and Walter says, 'I think I showed everyone in the road what I had got and told them who gave it to me.'

Foy came from Caithness Street, on the doorstep of the Tower Building and the Round Toll and its bars. O'Hara came from Lyon Street, just a bottle throw away. He had a brother Danny who died in the sinking of HMS *Hood*. In fact, many of the fighting men of the Twilight Zone did sterling service for their country in the Second World War. When researching this book with Walter Norval, one of the first memories he recounted to me was of the roll of honour displayed with pride on the wall in Duffy's Bar – just one of many bars which clustered, cheek by jowl, in the area and competed for business. The plaque commemorated the locals who had left to join the army and who had given their lives in the fight against Nazism. The area was fertile recruiting ground for the famous Scottish fighting regiments like the Black Watch, the Highland Light Infantry and the Seaforths. The roll of honour in Duffy's was a tribute to many brave men who, while they may have fought each other at home, died in bloody fields abroad doing their bit to stop the march of fascism across Europe.

During the war life was also grim for the folk still at home. Just a few miles down the road from the Round Toll, in Clydebank, air raids by Luftwaffe bombers, targeting the shipyards, had blitzed the crowded housing leaving only seven houses intact out of a stock of 12,000. The total number of Clydesiders to die in the air raids was 1,200 and, of those, 500 were from Clydebank. But such adversity brought out the best in the 'Bankies' as they were known. For the majority, life went on and the great ships continued to roll down the stocks to add to the arsenal Britain needed to take on the Germans. It wasn't the ideal climate for laughter but there was a tremendous community spirit and even Hitler's psychological weapon, the broadcasts of the traitor William Joyce, known as Lord Haw-Haw, couldn't undermine the spirit of the folk in the streets.

From his bunker in Germany, Lord Haw-Haw made a particularly odious and infamous broadcast to Britain on Radio Hamburg. In it, he drew attention to the slums, such as the Lyon Street ones, where he claimed the Glaswegians cowered in squalor, ten to room, with only outside toilets. Living conditions like those, he said, were precisely what was wrong with Britain under Winston Churchill. But the folk of Cowcaddens and Garscube Road had a ready response – laughter at this puffed up little traitor and his claims. Joyce, whose nickname came from his upper class drawl, eventually paid for his crimes when, after the war, he was arrested, tried and hanged in London.

As a young Norval began to get into serious crime, searchlights probed the sky over a Glasgow darkened by the blackout, the air-raid sirens wailed and the distant buzz of a Junkers bomber searching for targets beneath the deep dark clouds of the west of

Scotland was always a possibility. But even in the blackout of the blitz, street fighting was a way of life for many at night. The blacked-out streets were ideal places for the hard men who roamed the High Road. They offered cover for ambushes and made escape that bit easier. An ability to use your fists to good effect was an important asset in such a place but it was often a skill that had to be learned the hard way. The O'Hara brothers, for example, were schooled in fist fighting by their father who took them round to the back-courts at weekends, stripped them to the waist and encouraged them to knock the daylights out of each other as he looked on with undisguised approval.

Bare-knuckle ability could also be something of an earner. The various ballrooms had much need of bouncers to keep their punters, who'd spent many drouthy hours in the pubs before deciding to end the evening at the jiggin', under some form of control. This was a task regularly undertaken by Foy and O'Hara who stood guard at the door of the legendary Tower Ballroom at the Round Toll. The building still stands but the tower, that gave the place its name, is somewhat cut down and truncated these days and now looks pretty unspectacular. But, in its day, it was one of the most famous ballrooms in Glasgow and that, in itself, is an accolade. Its reputation was of a tough hall, the toughest in town, where fights were no surprise and where Foy and O'Hara had plenty of work for their fists.

Walter Norval recalls many hours spent in the snooker halls on the first two floors. He says, 'When the snooker closed we would go upstairs to the dance hall. Strangers were disliked . . . It was our place and we would annoy or fight with strangers. Every weekend there were fights – either with each other or we would get together to take on some youngsters from other districts who had come up to the dancing.' Walter tells of one occasion when a group of locals, older than he and the Wee Mob were, threw a guy from the fire escape of the dance hall, which was on the top storey, on to the ground below. 'He lay on the ground all weekend. I heard that rats had nibbled his feet and fingers but he survived,' says Norval – as ever a man unfazed by blood or gore.

Access to the Tower Ballroom was up a close – hardly the most glamorous of entrances. And toiling up the sixty-nine castle-like steps to the third floor must have been something of an effort on a sticky summer night but dancing played a major role in Glasgow life in those days. One of my *Glasgow Herald* colleagues Colm Brogan described dancing as 'almost a way of life' in his 1952 book *The Glasgow Story*. He wrote: 'Perhaps dancing provides an outlet for rumbustious and highly emotional people who chafe against inhibitions and conventions which they hardly know how to defy.'

An authority on dancing in Glasgow, Elizabeth Casciani, is not surprised by the fact that the Tower was on the top floor up a close. She is quoted as saying, 'anywhere they [Glaswegians] could find a space big enough to dance in, people would dance. Glasgow in the thirties was such a place of deprivation that dancing provided the glamour which people craved.' But she acknowledged that the subject might be a bit more complex as the passion for dancing was equally strong with the city's rich bourgeoisie, though they tended to patronise more up market halls like the Plaza, a south side institution that soldiered on into the nineteen nineties, the Dennistoun Palais de Dance and the Locarno in Sauchiehall Street. Dancing skills were taken so seriously that young people practised in local halls, such as the Tower, before taking their sequins and patent leather shoes to the big city centre halls.

The Co-op halls and even the City Bakeries promoted dances. Dance classes were a commonplace and the ability to dance was an necessary social skill. One famous musician who played the Tower was jazz trombonist George Chisholm who described to a local reporter the picture he retained of his early days on the bandstand there: 'There were those guys there who used to march about the floor keeping the best of order and shouting' – here he puts on his *Goon Show* voice – '"Nae burlin'!".'

A feature of the Tower that still remains is that fire escape at the back. This ended in mid–air half way up the first floor. Foy and the other chuckers-out found this helpful. Extreme bad behaviour would encourage them to huckle an offender to the ladder and let them find their way to the ground. When he got to near enough dancing age, Walter's status as a favoured son of the hard men who ran the door worked in his favour and he was allowed in. But it was not Norval behaviour to touch his forelock and thank his benefactors. No, he tended to skip round to the fire-escape door, surreptitiously open it and let his pals, who had shinned up the metal ladder, come in and join the fun. To Foy and O'Hara, this was taking liberties and O'Hara would grab Walter and inquire with little delicacy, 'Who the fuck let them in?' But John Foy, the king of all bouncers, would merely give Walter a clip on the ear, telling his young acolyte off in rough fashion. But behind it all were smiles and affection for this young Jack the Lad who, along with his Wee Mob, was hell bent on graduating to hard-man status and gaining the respect of the streets.

For young Norval and his pals, more serious matters than smuggling themselves into the 'jigging' loomed. Ahead were escapades on the road to realising an ambition – 'graduating' to borstal and early days behind bars in Barlinnie and Saughton. Another milestone was getting your name into the papers – something all red-blooded hoods enjoy even if they are reluctant to admit it. Down the years Walter Norval has featured in more than his share of lurid headlines. With his criminal lifestyle and a love life that attracted the tabloids, he helped to sell many a newspaper.

He has, however, developed a healthy scepticism on how the Glasgow press treats its gangland. Sometimes highly exaggerated tales exist to this day and contemporary gangland figures, like

Paul Ferris and the late Tam McGraw, find their every move covered by reporters who often have to rely on so-called inside information – and sometimes good old-fashioned imagination – to file their copy.

Speculation on the latest state of play in the turf wars among the Glasgow gangs sells papers and Walter has a classic example of exaggeration he likes to tell. One morning, as a teenager, he picked up his *Daily Record* – still the bible for followers of crime on the streets – to read the legendary column of Pat Roller telling of a gang fight at the Round Toll involving hundreds of Teddy boys and Garscube Road locals. It was presented as an amazing battle.

But the reality was not quite as amazing. According to Walter only around fifteen combatants were involved – five locals against ten Teddies. What had happened was that Walter and a few of his pals were standing around the Round Toll when the Teddy boys made the mistake of challenging them to a fight. Walter's mob were across the road in a flash and, helped by Foy who had been standing in a nearby close minding his own business, they waded into all and sundry. There could only have been one winner and the Teddies fled.

You still meet people on the Glasgow crime scene who insist they met Pat Roller – much to the amusement of the newspaper sub-editors who subtly changed the word patroller into that famous by-line. No such person as Pat Roller existed. The name was used nightly to head a column of crime briefs written as a daily task by whoever happened to be the late duty reporter. This unfortunate, toiling in the sweaty engine room of journalism, who started work around nine and stayed till perhaps five the next morning, spent his time phoning round the cop shops checking out the state of play on the streets that night.

This was long before the police had got themselves organised enough to have a well-manned press relations department to deal with inquiries. Today, every force – and Strathclyde is no exception – has highly trained, well-educated officers who specialise in liaising with TV and newspapers. Indeed, night after night, a modern news editor finds his desk awash with e-mails and faxes on the latest crimes – be they petty matters or desperate affairs where blood has been spilled or robberies in which thousands of pounds have been stolen. These days, even a burst water main gets the full e-mail/fax treatment.

But, on the night of The Battle of the Round Toll, we were still in the era when a reporter relied on the desk sergeant or whatever passing cop answered the phone to fill him in on the details. Most reporters also had a favourite cop who they cultivated down the years with a pint or two in the local or maybe a tip from the racing desk. Such police contacts often used the press to bolster their own reputations – though how a street rammy, involving Walter and his cronies and a few Teddy boys, came to sound like Custer's Last Stand is something of a mystery.

But the life of crime of Walter Norval was about to undergo a sea change. He was about to leave the relatively petty world of bricks through shop windows and street fighting to the more serious business of safe-cracking and armed robbery. Norval's war on the law was to move up a gear.

4

ROOFTOP RAMBLES
AND RATTLING TUMBLERS

The Wee Mob went out thieving almost on a nightly basis. It was a way of life and, like any other way of life, too much of the same becomes boring. Norval's boys were getting a little tired of the regular round of petty robbery on their own doorstep. A wider world beckoned – perhaps it was the visits to the Wee Phoenix picture house, with its diet of gangster films, that gave them aspirations to become involved in what they saw as the more glamorous kind of criminal activity. Cagney and Raft were their role models and *Angels with Dirty Faces*, in which Pat O'Brien, as the street-sharp priest with a big heart, persuaded Cagney to be dragged to the electric chair in fake terror in order to wean good Catholic boys away from a life of crime was a favourite.

But, in Hollywood terms, the Wee Mob were small beer indeed. Any thoughts of the big league or even graduating to a stretch in borstal or even the Bar-L were likely to require something more dramatic and adventurous than nicking sweeties from a factory. Flash cars, easy money and, eventually, guns were in the future. For now, the big city was just a tram ride down the road away and there were targets galore awaiting the attention of the would-be young robbers. Later in his criminal life, Walter Norval was to earn himself a reputation as a master-planner of robberies. He claims never to have made a move without thinking through what would happen when the plan was put into practice. He also claims never to have been caught, only 'betrayed'. Like a chess master, he preferred to think three or four moves ahead – at least.

Maybe this was because of his first really big attempt at robbery and what went wrong with it. Whatever the motivation was, the acquired knowledge that the most important matter of all was to line-up a foolproof plan of escape was instilled in his psyche. But that was certainly not a feature of the Wee Mob's first excursion deep into the territory where the city centre cops could provide a little more sophisticated opposition than that offered by old Dunky McSwan back on their home patch. Apart from figuring out that there were rich pickings to be had in some of the office blocks, this first expedition into the city centre was not blessed by much in the way of planning. All Walter and three of his pals from the High Road knew was that, after dark, entry to such a places was not much of a problem for a few fit young tearaways who could clamber up a rone pipe almost as easily as they could climb the tenement stairs. The three who accompanied Walter on this venture were Biggy, Joe and Johnny. All four had been in many a scrape together and were well known to the local cops. But now they were hell-bent on widening their criminal horizons.

After a reconnaissance trip or two into town, the teenagers made up their minds to target an office building in Hope Street, not far from the city's Central Station. Inexperienced, they had not taken into account that here, in the heart of the city, the beat cops out watching over the drunks and the travellers and the prostitutes, who lurked doing business in the dark lanes between the buildings around the stations, would be a little sharper than Dunky.

They waited till it was late and dark and, round the back of the building, the four pals found suitable rone pipes leading to the upper floors. They speedily and quietly shinned up the pipes, opened a window and scrambled into a deserted office. So far, it all seemed too easy and swiftly they trousered anything they could find – pens, lighters, money, notebooks. Any locked drawers were burst open and pillaged. At this stage in their careers, safes may well have been tempting but opening them was a skill the teenage gang had yet to learn – they simply didn't have the necessary expertise.

Just as the raid was getting into its stride, there was a sudden commotion in the street below – torches flashed, whistles sounded, men shouted. The noise of the police whistles was the real scarer. Every cop on the beat in these days relied on his 'Acme Thunderer', a standard issue, heavy duty police whistle that could make a piercing sound which would travel around 500 yards in the right conditions. It wasn't something you liked to hear if you were up to no good. The Wee Mob from the High Road panicked. As the cops entered the lane at the back of the building, Biggy was quick and smart enough to take to his heels and escape. But Walter, Johnny and Joe were trapped at the scene of the crime and the cops were nearing the door. The rogues reckoned that now the only way out was the way they had got in – through the broken window. But, clearly, descent to the streets was no option as the cops were waiting there. The villains would have to go up, in the hope that they could get on to the rooftops before the police, and escape into the darkness that way.

Johnny was first up the pipe, followed by Walter and Joe. But the leader in this climbing mission soon realised that he was at the top of the pipe all right but he wasn't on the roof. The rone pipe disappeared into a wall leaving the small matter of several feet or so of wall left to scale. It was too far for their arms to reach the coping round the roof. There was only one thing they could do. Walter clambered over Johnny on to his shoulders, reached up and, after some dangerous scrambling, made it to the roof that way. He then hauled his companions in crime up to join him. For whatever reason – perhaps they were needed at the scene of another break-in or at a gang fight or a late night mugging – the police down below disappeared almost as quickly as they had arrived.

The Wee Mob took stock. There may, indeed, be honour among thieves but there was certainly not what you could call trust – especially where the boys from the High Road were concerned. In the wee sma' hours, up in the cold dark of the roof, the Wee Mob searched one another to see who had looted the most cash. They lied to each other about how much actual money each had snatched in their brief looting of drawers and petty cash boxes. But, after much cursing and argument, the spoils were finally evenly distributed and it was decided to climb back down the rone pipe into the original office and to sleep on the floor till daybreak. At first light, that backbone of commerce, the office cleaner, arrived with bucket, mop and rags and opened the door. The Wee Mob were past her and down the stairs before she could blink.

With money in their pockets, the sixteen-year-olds waited for the pubs to open at 11 a.m. and headed for the nearest hostelry to blow the stolen cash on drink. Again, this was not the sort of move you would expect of the wily lawbreaker that Norval was to become but it was, perhaps, understandable on account of the youth of the boys and the excitement following the adventures of the night. The Wee Mob got blotto. In these days, the drinking age was eighteen but tough nuts like the Wee Mob looked old enough and hard enough to get what they ordered despite barmen's suspicions. Hard they were but, at this stage, not hardened drinkers and they were drunk in minutes. They were so noisy with it that they were eventually tipped out on to the street by the pub staff.

Regrouping, the trio decided to find another pub where, perhaps, the barmen were not so touchy and where some more drink could be obtained. The notion dawned on their befuddled brains that it might be an idea to steal a car to whisk them on to another dram shop. It wasn't a clever idea at all and the particular car they decided to steal compounded the error. The vehicle belonged to a man called Rab Conway who spotted them about to steal his pride and joy. Conway decided to take matters into his own hands and appeared, fists flailing and intent on making a citizen's arrest. He intended to march them to the police station and hand them over. The Wee Mob didn't take this lying down and a shovel, left handily in the street, was picked up and smashed on to Conway's head. As he staggered to his feet, the young thugs legged it to the safety of their closes in the Garscube Road.

But there was to be a twist in this tale. It turned out that certain Joe O'Hara of Lyon Street was one of Conway's uncles. The Wee Mob had made a bad tactical mistake. Joe O'Hara didn't take kindly to the idea of his relative being swatted on the head with a shovel by these would-be hard men. But the code of the streets saved them. The boys pleaded that the victim had not been sorting the matter out himself, by giving them a hiding, but intended taking them to the police. This was not the sort of behaviour O'Hara expected of his relatives and he contained himself enough merely to give the young villains a serious dressing down – a lucky escape indeed. It was not wise to fall foul of Foy or O'Hara. Or, indeed, mess about with the property of their relatives – even by accident.

In his teenage years, Walter remained close to Angie Jaconelli and she played an interesting role in one of his minor stings. His pal Biggy toyed with respectability at times and had, at one stage, even taken a regular job as the driver of a van delivering sweeties – still rationed and much in demand – to the local shops. Mind you, even this enterprise had a criminal side as he drove under an assumed name and lied about his age. One night in the pub, he let his Garscube Road drinking mates, including Walter, know that it had been a hard day on the delivery front and that he had not been able to complete his round. He moped over his beer that he had had to park the van nearby, with the delivery uncompleted and some sweets still inside and that he would have to be up at the crack of dawn the next day to catch up on the workload.

The next morning, with Mrs Norval away waitressing down the coast, young Angie had popped round to see that Walter was OK for breakfast and to give the house a quick tidy-up. As they lounged on a sofa, there was a knock on the door. In came Biggy in a state of some agitation and dismay and he proceeded to tell Walter and Angie that 'some bastard' had broken into his parked van and made off with the sweets. Walter started to dispense some sympathy for his mate but Biggy and Angie suddenly noticed that beside Walter's feet lay one sweet wrapper. After the crime, Walter had carefully tidied up the evidence of the sweet wrappers and destroyed them. However he had missed that one telltale wrapper and suddenly there was no mystery about who had done that particular night's thieving. Not for the first time, Walter Norval had turned a piece of inside information to his own ruthless advantage.

In 1945, with the war in Europe coming to an end, Walter's ambition to do a stretch in Polmont Borstal, and thereby underline his status on the streets as a hard man on the way up in the criminal world, was nearing fruition – as was the start of his career as an armed robber, though the weapon involved this time was just an air pistol disguised as something more powerful and frightening. Inside knowledge was again put to use.

But first the Wee Mob became involved in a spot of safe-breaking – or, to be more accurate, they became a safe-breaker's assistants. The word on the streets was that there was a tasty little safe to be had, complete with a bundle of cash, in an office near the Round Toll. Biadge Jaconelli was involved in this ploy and he reckoned they could get a safe-blower from town into the building to do the actual opening. The man they had in mind was a respected peterman called Green who could, for the right price, become available to rattle the tumblers or lay a little explosive in the right place. But first the thieves had to get into the building and this was deemed a suitable job for the Wee Mob.

Blocking the entrance to the office were strong vertical iron bars of a type still seen in many of the older buildings, in Glasgow, to this day. But the Wee Mob had the technology to deal with them. It was a situation in which something they called the 'bar stick' would be needed. This was a specially designed and strengthened metal bar, with a U-shape in the centre, that was manoeuvred in behind the bars. Its shape allowed a couple of strong young thieves, one at each end, to lever off the window guard. In the days before the installation of sophisticated electronic alarms, when bars were the only deterrent to stop thieves breaking in to premises, the 'bar stick' was a vital tool for the villain.

Breaking in to this office was the start of Walter and his mates making big money out of crime. When the safe was opened, there was a neat little haul of £500 to be picked out and, as payment for prising the office open, the Wee Mob were given a hundred pounds or so to split between them. This success encouraged the Wee Mob to break into a few other spots where there was a tempting safe. However, lacking the skills of the petermen from town, their solution was to lower the safe, on ropes, out of the window, take it to some lonely spot and then set about it with sledgehammers and cutters. The money often did emerge but the safe ended up looking like a sardine can that had been attacked by a hungry madman.

It was a hallmark of Walter's style to use tip-offs from insiders to point the way to where there might be a sum of money that was worth pinching. It was important to know when pay days and other times when safes would have cash in them were and getting hold of such information involved paying for it in cash or drink or a share of the spoils. And, as the episode of Biggy and the confectionery van showed, there was no law against cashing in on the knowledge of your pals and acquaintances.

Walter and the Wee Mob were by now enjoying nights at the dancing at the Tower and other ballrooms and the girls they picked up were, on occasion, to become unwitting sources of information. One of the gang, John H, met a girl called Susie at the Tower and Susie had a young friend, Sarah, who worked in a well-known tobacconist shop in the city centre. And, of course, in the back shop of this highly popular establishment stood a safe that was often stuffed with readies.

Walter and John H decided this was a turkey ripe for plucking. With a well-hidden fake pistol, they watched from an amusement parlour across the road till they saw Sarah and the boss add up the cash, put it in the safe and generally get ready for closing time. At the right moment, they skipped across the road, used the fear of the brandished gun to subdue the staff and pushed them aside. The shop blinds were pulled down and Sarah was forced to open the safe – though this time the haul was a mere £11. Walter took a supply of cigarettes to be delivered to their old mate Biggy who was doing some time in the Bar-L at the time. Unrecognised, the young robbers headed to the safety of their home streets and closes. At this stage, Sarah was unable to help the investigating detectives regarding the identity of the thieves.

The Wee Mob seemed to have got away with this first attempt at armed robbery. The raid on the tobacconist took place on 7 December 1945 and, that Christmas night, Walter found himself at Midnight Mass in St Joseph's, a landmark large Catholic church in the area. Not that this involved any sudden conversion to religion or the unthinkable thought of going straight – it was just curiosity and the urge to go along with his female company that night to the chapel. But, in there, he must have felt at peace with the world and fairly safe that he had escaped the clutches of the law after his move into armed robbery.

However, a severe shock awaited him on his return home to the Garscube Road flat. Some time before the robbery, John H's friend, Susie, had persuaded Walter and John to pose for a souvenir photograph at Jerome's, a famous and well-remembered city photographer of the day. Susie then proudly carried the snap in her handbag and somehow, weeks later, Sarah got a glimpse of it and recognised the guys who had robbed her shop. The game was up. Borstal and the real start of Norval's criminal life was only a short time and an appearance in Edinburgh High Court away.

5

BREAD AND WATER
AND A SPOT OF PORRIDGE

Before being tried for the tobacconist shop robbery, Walter was held in Barlinnie Prison or the Bar-L, as Glaswegians call that massive, old fashioned fortress in the East End. He had been taken there from Glasgow's Northern Police Office and, when the cell door clanged behind him for the first time, the man, who was destined to become Glasgow's first Godfather of crime, was no frightened teenager. His way of life, his inherent self-confidence and the barroom stories of his associates had all prepared him well for this moment. It was almost as if it was an inevitable right of passage for a career criminal, a man ambitious to go to the very top of the crime pinnacle in his city.

But, even if the Bar-L contained few surprises, some important lessons were there to be learned – like the ability to speak out the corner of the mouth when exercising in the prison yard. Until he was incarcerated in Glasgow's infamous prison for the first time, the young robber hadn't realised why, in the many prison films that he enjoyed watching so much, the stars, such as Cagney, Raft and Lancaster, talked out of the side of their mouths. This was an acquired skill to make sure the screws, as the prison officers are uniformly called, didn't know you were talking to another criminal and, just as importantly, didn't know what you were talking about. But, no matter how tough the prison officers were, no matter how determined they were to enforce the 'no talking' rule, as the prisoners trudged round the bleak yard in the bitter cold of the winter of 1945, the cons managed to converse and the latest information from the streets would be circulated as they exercised.

In this closed world, the cocky newcomer from the Garscube Road attracted attention. It was obvious that this was a man who was not in the least fearful of this grim place. There were no tears of loneliness, no hiding in his cell, no solitary dreaming of his freedom and promising himself to go straight the minute after his release. He was tough and he had a different agenda. The old lags teased him but Walter Norval is not a man who teases easily. His air of aggression and general lack of fear or respect for his new surroundings attracted the attention of one particular fellow inmate who knew a hard man when he met one.

While on remand in the Bar-L, Norval met a real old-fashioned gang leader for the first time. Jim Kemp, or 'Evil Jim', as he was known, was, in the Glasgow patios, a 'chib' merchant – that is, an expert with a knife and open razor – who ran the gangs and rackets of the Gallowgate, one of the toughest areas in the city. To control a place like that, it was necessary to be a handy man with an open razor. One man who could certainly claim that skill was Johnny Stark, the main character in a remarkable work of fiction, No Mean City, by Alexander McArthur and H Kingsley Long. Many people blamed this novel for blackening the name of the city, for tagging it forever as a city where, for generations, razor slashers walked the streets and terrorised locals and incomers alike. The 'cutting' was a way of life and lurid red scars on the face were worn like badges of honour.

Although it attracted much criticism, the portrayal of life in the Gorbals in the twenties and thirties in No Mean City was far from being an inaccurate picture. It is worth noting that the criticism of the novel mostly came, then and now, from politicians and others who refused to acknowledge the truth about Glasgow in these times, preferring to sweep it all under the proverbial carpet. It was as if the mayor of Chicago was convinced that the Mafia was a fictional organisation and life on the banks of Lake Michigan was as sweet as apple pie. In actual fact, of course, the infamous Chicago mayor, Big Jim Thompson, was part of the problem so perhaps there is something to be said for hiding your head in the sand!

The swaggering razor king that was the fictional Johnny Stark existed in real life – and there were plenty of them. 'Evil Jim', who could have played the role of Stark in any film version of the book, took a bit of a shine to young Walter. Kemp was in the Bar-L suspected of murder and, as an old hand in prisons, it was obvious to Kemp that Norval was destined for a longish spell in Polmont. The Wee Mob leader was too young for an adult prison but clearly he was the sort that needed to be behind bars and given a taste of the discipline for which the borstal system was notorious. Out of the side of the mouth, naturally, he gave Walter some helpful advice. 'When you go to Polmont tell Mr Bremner [one of the most important officers there at the time] that you know James Kemp.' As in all walks of life and on both the right and wrong side of the law, who you know can be important.

After a few weeks in the Bar-L, Norval found himself in Edinburgh High Court. His conviction for the armed robbery at the tobacconist was inevitable because of the positive identification. He was sentenced to three years and, without undue delay, the young robber found himself handcuffed to another convicted prisoner, taken out to the prison bus and on his way to borstal. John Lyon, the young man Walter was chained to, was, at twenty-one, just a few years older than he was. Lyon was convicted for his part in the stabbing of a navy man in a brawl in Washington Street in Glasgow city centre. Handcuffed together, they chatted on the way to the police bus with its darkened windows.

Walter wanted to know what Polmont Borstal, which was to be his home for the next three years, was really like and assumed that a fellow, such as the one he was shackled to, would know. But his companion, young John Lyon, had other matters much more desperate than a spell in borstal on his mind. In court that fateful day, his appeal against a death sentence had finally been turned down. In a matter-of-fact style, Lyon mentioned to the young armed robber that 'they are going to hang me in fortnight'. Young Walter took this with a pinch of salt until a warder confirmed the destiny that awaited the man on the other end of the 'cuffs. More than sixty years later, Walter remembers the killer – who made some sort of criminal history as the first person to die on the gallows in Barlinnie's new hanging shed in 1946 – as calm, resigned and brave in the face of death. Such a close brush with a man bound for the rope did not, however, steer Walter away from a life of crime and a lifelong fascination with firearms and violence. He just couldn't get the message that crime and violence doesn't pay – not even when talking to man a few days away from the gallows.

The borstal regime was designed to get that message across to the youngsters with a mixture of tough (on occasion brutal) discipline and the hard labour of working on the prison farm or at a factory bench – something of a new experience for many of the young inmates. The borstal system was a precursor of the boot camps so beloved of extreme right-wing politicians today. But, if what happened in the borstal establishments is anything to go by, any attempt to reintroduce such a regime under another guise is doomed to failure. Borstal did nothing to turn Norval away from a life of crime – indeed, it seems to have hardened his attitude and, with a few exceptions, turned him against the very people who were supposed to be trying to help him.

Norval's is not a lone voice in condemning the borstal system. Even in its heyday, it was much criticised in the liberal press and many, who survived the system, came out into the real world to condemn it and its brutality. Walter had an early introduction to the depths that such brutality could sink – literally. When behind bars, Norval was often a troublemaker and ready to fight at a moment's notice. In Polmont Borstal, this behaviour was often punished with a spell in the 'digger'. These were special punishment cells, deep below ground which were damp and dark and reached by a narrow flight of stairs. Down in these degrading surroundings, there were other deprivations like a restricted diet and the occasional visit from a demented screw who took out his spite on life and the inmates by giving them a going over with fist and boot. There are many tales of life in such an institution that horrify when looked back at from today's more liberal perspective.

Some lads got an early taste of what to expect when the first inmates to arrive were pulled out of the prison van by their hair. For one, the most significant experience of his first day was an officer punching him in the face breaking his nose. So-called education in the early borstals was simply a morning of silence and remaining absolutely still. Along with physical training, the inmates received training in 'slopping out', the disgusting morning ritual of emptying chamber pots they'd had to use since lock-up time the night before because their cells had no toilets. If the idea was to steer youngsters away from a life of crime, it just didn't work for Walter Norval or for hundreds or others like him – quite the reverse. On his release, he was able to tell his hero John Foy that not only had he been in the Bar-L, he had survived borstal too. He felt good. Walter Norval claims that, for him, surviving borstal was like winning a medal. His street cred and reputation as a hard man had been given a boost by a naïve system that was allegedly designed to push youngsters like him back on to the straight and narrow. So much for rehabilitation.

However, during the long months before he could once again strut down the Garscube Road, Walter tasted the worst that borstal could offer. His initial reaction was to realise that the whole ethos of the place was to knock, often literally, discipline into the inmates. Blind obedience to the rules was the aim, regardless of how pointless or counter productive the rules were.

Walter's first two months were spent in 'B' hall, where the new inmates were schooled in the ways of the institution, before being moved to a more permanent billet inside the high walls and fences. He was as quick to make his mark as the prison officers were quick to assess him. One warder, called Fullerton, observed accurately to him that, 'You're not a hard case – you're a head case!' The cells were sparse with wooden floors and just a locker and a bed. But they were spotless. The whole place was spotless – so clean 'the flies were afraid to come in the window', remembers Walter. The warders would even turn tables upside down to check that the unseen side was as pristine as the table top.

This level of cleanliness was easily achieved. Almost from the moment of arrival, the inmates were down on their knees floor-scrubbing which was a bullying ritual that was designed to take the spirit out of even the toughest teenager. The boys were lined up, in precise order, on their knees, and the warders kicked buckets of water across the floor to them. To be a 'screw' in a borstal, you needed the voice and bearing of an army sergeant major. Commands were screamed out at the top of voices and 'Soap on brush!', 'Water on!' 'Scrub!' would echo round the halls. When one section was scrubbed, the boys were ordered on to an overlapping section. This was achieved by more shouting – 'Move to the right!' 'Move to the left!'. And that was the routine, day after day, hall after hall, corridor after corridor. Not an inch of floor was left unscrubbed. And so the spirit was knocked out of the boys till they were on their knees – spiritually as well as physically.

Eventually, the inmates were assigned to other tasks – in the shoe shop, the farm or, as in Walter's case, the kitchen. On the streets, Walter found no difficulty in making enemies but, during his many periods of incarceration, he was always adept at making useful friends. His surprising innate cheerfulness seemed to work in his favour whether in a borstal, an army prison or in such grim penal fortresses as Peterhead or Barlinnie. In the kitchen at Polmont, things were no different and he struck up a relationship with Mr Lowe, the cook. Lowe had trained as a chef in civvy life and was always willing to pass on a little of his expertise to any lad willing to learn.

For Walter, being assistant to the cook was an attractive billet. He enjoyed his food and, by working in the kitchen, there was always the chance of some little extra rations. But it was hard work – especially preparing the breakfast which was porridge, naturally! He was up at 4.30 a.m. to make a start on the meal. As well as the vast tureens of porridge to be stirred, three hundred slices of bread had to be buttered. Just stirring the porridge took some strength so large were the quantities in each pot. And then there was the cocoa to get ready. The porridge was, of course, heavily salted – no namby-pamby little spoonfuls of sugar with this stuff.

The boys were marched into the dining hall where they had to stand at attention, totally still, as they waited for the unappetising fare to be served. Hundreds were fed at a time. The milk for the porridge was doled out with military precision and a brief grace was said – 'Heavenly father, giver of everything good and perfect, we thank you. Amen.' The nod in the direction of religion was, no doubt, a good and desirable thing but the choice of grace less than appropriate considering what was about to be consumed.

A highlight in the kitchen was the procedure of making the soup for the day – the one thing on the menu guaranteed to meet with the favour of hungry lads. However, before the soup, there was more emphasis on cleaning and polishing – and, of course, there was the little matter of washing hundreds of porridge bowls, side plates and cocoa mugs with no gleaming dishwasher to tackle them. But, in a borstal, there were two things that were not in short supply – manual labour and time – and the washing up was done by the boys, bent over the sinks and wielding a natty tea towel. The seven giant pots, sticky with the residue of the porridge, were a major test. Once they were clean inside, they and their lids were polished to a state where you could have used them for mirrors.

Apart from the soup, the food was mostly unappetising. The kitchen baked its own bread and made 'hard cast', a sort of biscuit. Mince was a staple of the main meal of the day though, in Walter's opinion, even the most highly skilled forensic scientist would have found it a challenge to detect the meat in it. The chef gave Walter full reign in the preparation of the vegetables for the pease meal soup, Scotch broth or lentil soup. Stirring the massive quantities of ingredients in the huge cauldrons was just as good exercise as any work out in the gym.

But, frugal as the diet was, there were occasions when it could appear to be as attractive as a restaurant meal in town. Walter, on occasion, found himself in the aforementioned notorious 'digger', that special underground cell in the punishment block. Give cheek to a screw or fall out of line in any way and three days' solitary in the 'digger', on a diet of bread and water, was the official punishment. However, the punishment often also took an unofficial turn with warders grabbing a troublemaker's head and holding it between his knees while beating him up around the ribs. On other occasions, the warders would simply lash out with their fists.

There was a culture of violence on both sides of the divide in a place like borstal. Inmates often heard the screams of alleged troublemakers being beaten up by the staff. The danger of sudden violence breaking out between healthy young men caged and tormented by the regime was an everyday possibility. But the system provided a possible way round any disputes. If you were at loggerheads with another inmate over some perceived slight or other, you asked the warders for permission to have a 'square go' with him. A suitable room was used as an impromptu boxing ring and the warders provided gloves, held the jackets and watched as the rivals battered the daylights out of each other. This was much preferable to letting disputes fester with the possibility of youngsters stealing knives and stabbing each other – or, worse, attacking an officer.

Walter put this system to good use to build his status in the institution. Homosexuality was another problem and any youngsters who didn't have the right macho image were always at risk. There was bullying both in uniform and out of it in borstal and, in Walter's time, one inmate in particular made a habit of teasing and touching one lad who didn't have the spirit or strength to fight back. To offer him some protection, Walter got the lad to sit near him in the dormitory but more than this was required. Walter decided the bully needed taking down a peg. He reported to an officer saying, 'Norval 4203, permission to fight.' This was how the system worked – both parties gave their numbers to the screws and a battle was arranged.

Walter's pal from the Wee Mob, John H, was with him in borstal and he worried that Walter had gone too far this time. His opponent was a much feared hard case who had a reputation as a dangerous battler. This particular inmate was far from the toughest in the institution. Older, more long-term prisoners were worse but he was definitely no pushover. 'You'll be killed,' was John H's pre-fight prediction. No so. Walter tore into action with such speed and ferocity that he felled his opponent with his first blow – a punch to the throat. The bully had got his comeuppance. This one fight was enough to secure Walter such a reputation that no one ever challenged him in the makeshift ring and it won him some respect from the older hard cases.

Boxing wasn't the only sport on offer for the inmates. They had a football team that was good enough to take on amateur teams from nearby Falkirk and win. Such matches allowed the boys to get rid of their energy and show their prowess. Walter particularly enjoyed these outings. He had always been a skilful footballer and some, who watched him play, commented that he would have made a good professional. Most of the spectators were warders who were there to make sure their charges didn't do a runner. Playing football in such circumstances must have been quite an experience for the local lads.

But, for the inmates of Polmont Borstal, such outings were merely brief respites from the cruel regime of bullying and days filled monotonously with a mixture of work and physical training. In the darkness of night, in the various dorms and cells in this unlamented place, the sound of youngsters crying themselves to sleep was commonplace. The regime, however, couldn't break every youthful spirit. Humour did, occasionally, shine through and sometimes brains, unstretched by the regime, could still be inventive. Perhaps the only positive memory of borstal, etched on the mind of Walter Norval, is what he calls the Borstal Song. Who wrote it or when he doesn't know. But the words are a poignant insight into the mind of a youngster sent to this place. And they serve as a reminder that the borstal experience was only the beginning of a life of crime for many who did time within its walls. They should also act as food for thought for those in the twenty-first century who bay for the return of boot camps and bullying.

THE BORSTAL SONG

I'm a lad who done wrong,
Very wrong in his time.
It was company that led me astray.
And, like many a youth,
I was led into crime,
And to borstal they sent me away.
I once got a job in a dockyard,
Beside some old pals that I know,
But, while working one day,

My foreman did say,
'My lad you must pack up and go.
You're a jailbird, I know,
So pack up an go,
For jailbirds we do not employ.'
I said, 'Give me a chance to be honest,
Give me a chance, won't you, please?
For, if luck's in my way,
I may find it some day,
'Cause I am out on my Ticket of Leave!

Such a ditty, sung at night by the inmates in darkened dorms, would bring a tear to a glass eye, to use the old Glasgow phrase.

But the epitaph and the reality of borstal are much harsher by far. Few left that place with a spirit of optimism and a desire to go straight. The brutality and the bullying were not effective methods of sorting out young men who had spectacularly jumped the rails and abandoned the rules of an honest life for a life of crime. Walter Norval and other intelligent, but flawed, youngsters who had found themselves in borstal look back and label the regime a failure. And, when Walter finally left Polmont, to be put on the train back to Glasgow and his destiny on the streets, he dramatically and nastily signalled his lack of respect for borstal and its warders. As the carriage slowly pulled away, heading to Glasgow's Queen Street Station, he spat in the face of his escort.

6

THE BAD SOLDIER NORVAL

It was like a scene from a Hollywood horror film or a gritty documentary on madness in some remote Siberian prison camp. A high wire fence, topped with jagged barbed shreds, created a secure compound around a vegetable garden that was mostly filled with cabbage and lettuce. Caged behind these high wire walls, a ragged figure, unshaven and unkempt, in dirty trousers and vest, laboriously picked caterpillars by the handful from the cabbages and the lettuce and placed them on the blade of his spade. Then, wild-eyed, he ground them to a green greasy pulp with a stone.

Mad it may have looked to the spectators watching this ugly scene. Village girls and their army boyfriends gazed through the wire mesh at the infamous Mad Scotsman of Donnington Army Prison Camp in 1948. But this was Walter Norval in calculating mode rather than in genuine madness. And those calculations were all about how to get his 'ticket' out of the army.

In the first instance, the army had experienced some difficulty in getting their hands on Walter to give him the privilege of a couple of years national service. The timing was wrong. Walter had hated, with a deep loathing, the bullying discipline of borstal. A leader rather than a follower, he arrived back in Glasgow off the train from Polmont in the mood to pick up life with the Wee Mob, to start giving orders again rather than taking them and to have some normal time with his teenage compatriots. His number one priority was to make up for time spent behind the walls of an institution he had grown to hate. But there was a small problem. In these days, with the Second World War not long ended, young men were expected to register for national service when they reached the age of eighteen. If they passed the medical this meant they would spend a little more than two years in either the army or the air force. (To qualify for national service in the Royal Navy, you had to register early to express your preference and you also had to join the Royal Naval Volunteer Reserve for a year or so before you were due to be called up.)

There was widespread disregard for the need to register and many a bolshie youth refused to do so and got away with it, particularly in Glasgow and the rougher areas of all Britain's cities. But, if you were over age and in borstal and you had neglected to register, the game was up – the authorities had you in their hands. There was no escape from the army. You had to serve part of your borstal sentence first and, after that, you were given three days at home to sort out your affairs. Then it was off to the barracks for assessment and training and into the coarse khaki uniform to serve your time as a military man. You could also expect to have your character moulded for the good by a couple of years of discipline.

Well, that was the theory. In the case of young offenders like Walter, you simply moved from one institution where discipline and blind obedience were the order of the day to another. This was an arrangement that didn't meet with the approval of young Norval who was back in the Garscube Road and thirsty for the life of a free man. It was nothing new to him to be wary of the attention of Glasgow's finest in blue uniforms but now the enemy was twofold – the city's own cops and the military police would be on the look-out for him. It was to be the first of many spells on the run from the military police. He had been sent to Edinburgh, under escort, from Polmont to be given a medical before starting his national service. He passed the medical and was then allowed to go back to Glasgow for three days to sort out his affairs. After this, he was required to report for army duty but, despite the fact that doing his spell of national service would have knocked a year off his borstal sentence, Walter was in no mood to serve king and country.

On his return to the streets, he had received a psychological blow. There were rumours about his mother and a character known in the Twilight Zone as Joe the Pole. This was a man named Joe Kotarba and he was much younger than Eva. Kotarba, like many Polish soldiers, had come to Scotland and stayed on after the war. Walter first set eyes on him when he accompanied Eva on a visit to borstal. But, as mother and son talked, the Pole was merely a man in the background, mysterious, silent and unexplained. On his release, Walter's friend Dunky White, who, by this time, had married Angie Jaconelli, dropped hints to Walter about the nature of Eva's relationship with this unlikeable man. Angie confirmed it. From the start Walter was sure the liaison, which was to end in marriage and tragedy, was merely a ploy by the Pole to get his hands on Eva's cash.

Walter instantly decided that the Pole was not stepfather material or as he put it 'He's no gonnae be my da'.' Walter put the word out to the Pole that he should keep away. It was advice Kotarba didn't take and he would live to regret it. Around this time, Walter began to do some serious 'winching', as Glaswegians describe courting, of his own with Ina McCormick, the niece of John 'The Bull' McCormick of canal-side fighting fame. Nights at the pictures, fish teas, card schools, talking long into the wee small hours in room and kitchens. For a young man on the run, it was a short time of what passed for normal life after borstal.

But it was only to last a month or so. The cops on the beat knew that Walter was hiding from the military police and every move he made was thought out beforehand to make sure the legendary detective Joe Beattie, then on the beat in the Garscube Road area, and his colleagues didn't spot him. But on this, the first of many spells on the run from His Majesty's armed forces,

Walter was to taste a particularly bitter betrayal. Eva asked him round to her house one night 'for a clean shirt' and a fry-up for tea. In all innocence, her young son took the invitation at face value and turned up for the treat. He was hardly in the house when the doorbell rang. It was the military police. He had been 'coppered' by his own mother who, Walter suspects, wanted him out of the way so that there would be an end to his threats towards Joe the Pole which would allow her to get on with her romance.

He was taken to the guardroom at the old Maryhill Barracks, barely a mile or so from his present home. Nowadays, as he makes his way from his home to the shops, pubs and betting shops of Maryhill Road, the old barracks wall is a daily reminder of that time. He spent ten days in the bleak Glasgow barracks and then he was posted to Richmond in Yorkshire. The camp he was sent to was familiar to thousands of young Scots who began their national service there. After the initial six weeks of training, the intention was to assign Walter to a regiment, the Green Howards, but, in the event, they never saw him. Indeed, of the almost two and a half years he was supposed to spend in national service, he only spent nineteen days as an ordinary soldier – some kind of record, you'd have to suspect. The rest of the time he was on the run or in jail – either civil or military. It was a dangerous and adventurous time.

Army life at Richmond was not to Walter's taste. He could not stomach the regime, the constant discipline, the poor food, the lack of privacy, the need to jump to attention when told and the unquestioning need to respond to any order immediately, regardless of whether or not it made any sense. It was too much to take and too much like the institution he had just left in Scotland. It seemed to him this was borstal all over again – except he was in an army uniform. He stuck it for one long miserable week. Then he simply left the barracks and took the train north to Glasgow Central Station.

Back home, he took up with John Harris of the Wee Mob. They needed money and their idea of 'earning a living' was a succession of thieving excursions to warehouses, pubs and shops. They were out almost every night of the week and the rich pickings were easy to dispose of through bookies or publicans anxious to turn a dollar on the black market. Fencing the stuff was not a problem. Clothes rationing, which had begun during the Second World War in 1941, was still in force and you also needed coupons to buy sweets and even for staples like tea and sugar. Rationing created some desperate shortages that played right into the hands of men, such as Walter, whose stolen goods would be sold on the black market.

To today's well-fed Glaswegians, the thought of living on two ounces of tea and two ounces of sugar a week, plus an egg a month and a wee pat of butter must seem almost unbelievable. When they first began to appear in the shops, fruits, such as bananas, were gazed on in wonder and a chicken was a rare treat. The creation of such shortages was a powerful driving force for the underworld of the time. An egg or two took on a surprising cash value simply because of the forces of supply and demand.

Whisky, too, always an important lubricant in Glasgow life, was also in short supply and, therefore, a favourite target for thieving dockers who could sell any bottle they could get their hands on. The criminal of today is quite likely to plan an enterprise over a decent claret and celebrate its success in champagne. In the forties, the working man was reduced to taking the one whisky a week that the bar would serve him and saving it in a bottle to make sure that, when Hogmanay came around, there was at least a dram or two to share. The black market price for sugar, eggs, tea, etc. was four times the ordinary price. Clothing coupons and bales of cloth also attracted a huge prices and bookies, who had readies and the desire to dress well, were particularly likely to pay the inflated prices for these commodities.

Being on the run from the military police was no big deal since Walter and his mates were effectively on the run from the City of Glasgow police on a permanent basis. Although his nights were spent out on the prowl, he still found time to carry on his romance with Ina. He met her for meals after she finished work and there were card sessions of pontoon, solo, rummy and whist and a game or two of 'fat', a card game much favoured in jails. While Walter plied his nefarious trade after dark, his bride-to-be had a good honest job serving in one of Glasgow's many grocer's shops – McBride and Blacks, now long forgotten.

But Norval's escape from Richmond was to be short lived and, after about a month, he was spotted on the streets and rearrested. He was given ten days in the familiar surroundings of the old Maryhill guardroom and then posted to Hillsea Barracks in Portsmouth. And, there, fate played one of the tricks that it seems to reserve for those destined for an incident-packed life. Who should he meet but his old mate and companion in crime Dunky White, the man who married Angie.

Putting two such characters together away from home and in a barracks where security could have been tighter was not a good idea. At this stage in their military careers, both young Scots may have been in uniform but they were untrained and still without flashes on their khaki garb to indicate a regiment or status. They were the rawest of the raw and restless for excitement. Walter suggested a night in the local taverns. 'Where will we get the money for that?' wondered the naïve Dunky.

As always, Walter had a scheme. 'Cheesecutter' hats, to be worn by the squadies when in their best uniforms, were at a premium at Hillsea. Walter knew most of his mates had one in their lockers and he knew that such hats could be sold round the barracks for a tidy profit. For some unfathomable reason, there seems to have been a shortage of this desirable headgear in this particular establishment. '"Tan" the lockers,' he instructed Dunky. His companion in crime wondered how that might be done but Walter had already thought it out. He told Dunky that, when the trainee storemen, who shared their dorm, returned that night he would divert them to the NAAFI canteen with some cock and bull story of a meeting they had been ordered to attend. While they were at the canteen and otherwise occupied, the lockers could be broken into in safety. And, indeed, that is exactly what happened.

But, the next morning, Walter and Dunky were under suspicion. Smooth talking as ever, Walter told his inquisitors that he had had nothing to do with it – why on earth should they suspect him? He had been in the NAAFI canteen with the other soldiers. It was pointed out that it was odd that only one locker in the dorm had escaped the attention of the thief – Walter Norval's. Dunky got a verbal 'doing' for his stupidity but, on this occasion, the duo got away with it.

The cash collected from the sale of the 'Cheesecutters' went on a night in local pub, the Red Lion, and after a serious number of pints an acquaintanceship was struck up with an Englishman who was a cook at the barracks and who didn't seem to realise the sort of men he was dealing with in these two Scots from the Garscube Road. Filled with beer and bonhomie the cook told the duo that, if they went to a certain room next morning, they would be rewarded with a full breakfast delivered by himself. This was, indeed, something to look forward to and, the next morning, Walter and Dunky, hung-over but hungry, waited for the promised little treat. But it never came and they eventually had to repair to the canteen for lunch. Who should be dishing out the meals but the big talker of the night before. He got his reward – a plate of mince and tatties, smack bang in the face, followed by a vicious swinging punch that floored him. For Walter, too, there was a reward. He was packed off to jankers for a day or two peeling potatoes.

It was inevitable that the pair would take off again and they soon found themselves back on the run in Glasgow.

On 2 September 1947, in the midst of all this mayhem and constantly dodging two sets of police, military and civil, Walter and Ina tied the knot in the less than glamorous surroundings of Glasgow's Martha Street registry office. In Scotland, the banns for a wedding, civil or religious, have to be posted at least three weeks before the wedding. Doing this was a risk that Walter had to take if he wanted to be married and they had the banns posted in the city centre, some distance from the patch of the cops from the Garscube Road area, who were on the look out for the serial escaper. And there was no danger of the best man, John Harris, his friend from the borstal days, letting the cat out of the bag!

Martha Street is something of a Glasgow icon. Standing just off the famous George Square and near the huge Victorian pile that is the City Chambers, it was the scene of countless weddings down the years – it was really the only choice for those who spurned a church wedding either through lack of religious conviction or lack of cash. The walls of the corridors were white tiled and the many rooms, used to record births marriages and deaths as well as wedding ceremonies, were painted in dull institutional colours. The staff toiled over huge ledgers, recording the lives of Glasgow's citizens – from the good and the great to the lowest of the low – in immaculate copperplate handwriting. With its old-fashioned inkwells, brown folders and dusty filing cupboards, it was a place that had a distinctly Dickensian atmosphere.

It was an unimposing setting for a wedding but it was also a building that, at some time or other, touched the lives of most Glaswegians. And, since many a wedding there was a 'shotgun' affair, there is some serendipity in that the building itself is almost on the doorstep of the old maternity hospital! There was no swanky party after the wedding bash for Walter and Ina. Nor an exotic honeymoon in the sunshine and sand of some Spanish resort. Life was more basic in these days. After the civil requirements and all the attendant form-filling was over, the wedding party repaired to the Gaumont cinema, in Sauchiehall Street. It is now no longer in existence but, at that time, it was one of the top attractions in the city centre.

Opposite it was another legendary Glasgow cinema, La Scala, which was famous for its 'golden divans' – a sort of sofa-style seating for which you paid a premium and in which much groping took place between sweating and panting Glasgow teenagers as the Hollywood stars flickered across the silver screen unwatched. The Gaumont, too, had its own special attraction, what, in today's jargon, would be called its 'unique selling point' – a tea-room. Here, the wedding meal was served and, afterwards, Walter and his party trooped in to watch the current hit film.

After the wedding, Walter got rooms for a time in High Craighall Road and later in Eagle Street and attempted to lead as normal a life as possible as a married man but nothing was ever really normal in the early years of the life of the Godfather-to-be.

On the streets of the Twilight Zone, it was criminal business as usual for Walter and his pals but this nightly round of 'tanning' shops and businesses was a high-risk enterprise and the very regularity of it, and the occasional need to be out on the streets during the daylight hours, meant that it had to end eventually. Just before he was rearrested, Walter once again proved that he was an elusive and difficult man hold on to. He had been talking to his mentors Foy and O'Hara and some other hard men from Garscube Road on the corner of Caithness Street – a somewhat cocky move for a man on the run. However the cosy chat ended in a Keystone Cops scene when a constable called Fisher, new to the patch and keen to make a name, recognised Walter and attempted to handcuff him. But he was left holding Norval's coat when the renegade soldier wriggled out of it and legged it to safety. PC Fisher, like the legendary Joe Beattie and many other cops on the Garscube Road beat, now had first-hand experience of the difficulty of pinning Walter Norval down.

The late Joe Beattie, who was to go on to play a major role in the trapping of Glasgow's infamous mass murderer, Peter Manuel, in the late fifties, had plenty of experience of Norval's slipperiness. On one occasion, no doubt in response to a tip off, he landed up, around midnight, banging the door of the flat he and Ina shared. He urged Walter to give himself up, bellowing, in best 'B'-movie style, 'Come out, Wattie – I know you are in there!'. He then informed the folk behind the door he was prepared to wait all night if necessary. Inside, they jammed the door and prepared to sit it out. The snag was that the lavatory was out on the stair-head and, to reach it, you had to leave the flat. As Beattie listened and shouted through the letter box that he could hear them whispering, a basin and old newspapers were pressed into service. In the end, the cop gave up and left around five a.m. Sometimes it just isn't worth it.

Another episode emphasised how tricky Dunky and Walter were to catch. They were sharing adjacent rooms on the second floor of a tenement. By now, Walter had already developed the wariness and forward planning that were to be his hallmark and so he looked for an escape route – just in case. A rone pipe, that ran down between the windows of the two rooms, offered an ideal emergency exit. Should circumstances dictate it, they could slide down the rone pipe and escape to safety.

However, when this emergency exit was called into use, Dunky, never quite as sharp as his friend, was to live up to his reputation for slow-wittedness in a somewhat hilarious fashion. The lads had been playing cards, with a few others, late at night in Dunky's room. Dunky was getting tired and decided to have a nap but, rather than stop the game, he went through to Walter's room. A loud battering at the door announced the arrival of the police, seeking the two deserters. Walter, remembering that he was in Dunky's room and that the rone pipe would now be on a different side from where it was relative to his own room, leapt out the window, grabbed the pipe and slid himself down it. As he was making his way to the ground, a body hurtled past him.

On wakening, Dunky had forgotten they had switched rooms and had jumped out on the wrong side of the window, missing the rone pipe and going straight down into the back court and landing painfully 'on his arse', as Walter puts it.

Nonetheless, on this occasion the two made good their escape. Walter went into hiding at his Aunt Maggie's in Hamilton Hill and Dunky eventually ended up in Angie's place in Sawmillfield Road. A week later, though, Dunky was caught and, three weeks after that, Walter, too, was arrested in the flat, leaving him wondering, to this day, if Angie, just like his mother before her, had 'coppered' them, as he puts it.

Walter was court-martialled in Aldershot and sent to Colchester military prison for three months. This was no easy stretch, even for a young man who had experienced the tough conditions of Barlinnie and borstal. He spent much of the time in the 'wet cell', a dank and malodorous place reserved for hard cases. His refusal to do everything 'at the double' or run around with heavy packs on his back meant he spent many extra hours in the punishment cells and, for long spells, he was given the unwanted task of emptying the evil-smelling toilet cans that had been filled, during the night, by the hapless inmates of this grim place. In this primitive prison, the inmates were graded for behaviour and privileges were granted to those with the reputation of conforming and giving the least trouble. True to character, Walter was accorded Stage One status, the lowest of the low, but, again true to character, he managed to lean on a fellow Scot, with Stage Three status, to get parcels of food and tobacco passed surreptitiously to him. This was important as tobacco was – as it still is in most prisons – the jail currency for the inmates and it could be used to grease away some of the hardships of a stretch in Colchester.

You might think that, after Colchester, the army would have realised that Walter Norval was a hopeless case and given up trying to turn him into a storeman or a sweeper up. By this time, you might have expected it would have been easier for them to just discharge him. But, no. Initially, they sent him to Bramley in Kent. He was en route for Donnington in the north of England and, surprisingly, the serial deserter was given a railway pass to transport himself north – not a wise move. The ticket was for travel from London to Donnington but Walter simply altered the destination to Glasgow, initialled it himself, in the name of a fictional captain, and, once again, headed home.

Amazingly, he got away with it. When he showed the ticket collector the altered pass, the railwayman seemed to accept it at first. But, because the destination on the pass had been changed, the collector became suspicious and came back, later in the journey, to request another look at the pass. Walter sweet-talked the ticket collector into believing that he, the ticket collector, had been given the pass to keep on his first visit and that he himself must have lost it. The hapless railwayman then filled in a slip for payment for the extra part of the journey and Walter signed it. On arrival at the Central Station in Glasgow, there was more drama. Walter realised that his uniform, without flashes or regimental identification, would attract the attention of any military police who might be there. But, luckily for him, there were some Scots soldiers returning from Germany on the train and they agreed to let Walter march through the ticket gate with them and so within the safety of their group, the give-aways of his uniform were hidden from prying eyes. It worked.

But he didn't get away scot free. Just to show that British bureaucrats are as good as any in the world, Walter got a letter, some time later, asking him for ten shillings and sixpence for the extra bit of the rail fare from Donnington to Glasgow. Back on the run in Glasgow, it was soon a return to the nightly routine of breaking and entering business premises, stealing anything he could lay his hands on and selling the loot on the black market.

By now, life on the run was almost routine. The fact that clothing coupons were still at a premium had no effect on Walter or Dunky, who was also on the run from the army. When you regularly break into tailors' shops, getting hold of some decent clothes is not a problem. The pair had, what they termed, great success with a major raid on a big-name tailor's shop in Glasgow city centre.

But Dunky made another of his spectacular, almost comical, mistakes that, once again, showed that his criminal brain was no match for that of his friend. It was around New Year and, in Scotland, at that time, New Year was a holiday of much greater importance than Christmas. At New Year, everything shut down but at Christmas-time the giving of presents, the visits to the kirk and the family gatherings had to be made to fit in with the working pattern. In those days, most men would get out of bed on 25 December and head off for yet another day of toil.

Of course, work was not a major concern for Walter or Dunky but New Year, on the other hand, was significant – for Walter, in particular. For the past four years, at this special time of Scottish celebration, which, naturally, involved huge drinking sessions at home and in the pubs, he had either been in a jail or in some other institution. He had, therefore, missed out on the singing of Scots songs, the swilling of beer in the warm pubs of Garscube Road, the glowing lights spilling out on to glistening frosty pavements. So, having the chance of a Hogmanay to remember, even if it involved that other Scottish tradition – the all day hangover of 1 January – was tempting. Walter should have been wary of taking to the streets with so many cops on the look out for him. But no, he determined to have a good New Year in the Round Toll Bar – hardly a wise choice for a man on the run. Dunky went with him and was even less circumspect. He was resplendent in a suit and shirt stolen from the tailor's he had raided with Walter. And, inevitably they were spotted and it was back into Barlinnie while the authorities worked out what to do next with this pair of desperadoes.

Throughout his criminal career, behind bars and on the streets,

Walter has tended to side with the underdog, attach himself to the bullied and take out the bully – although it has to be acknowledged that, to rule a criminal gang, you have to be something of a bully yourself and fearsome fists and the ability to spill blood do come in handy when you are giving orders to hard men. Walter could also talk a good game in any court. On this occasion, Walter and Dunky appeared from Barlinnie before a Glasgow Sheriff called Boyd Berry, a well-known figure on the bench who had earned himself the nickname of 'The Borstal King' because of his belief that a stretch in such an establishment would straighten out any youngster. Being a realist, Walter pleaded guilty but, with his passion for helping the underdog, he spoke out strongly in favour of Dunky who had decided to plead not guilty. In his version of events, Walter told the court he had done the thieving and sold the 'gear' to his pal. Glasgow Sheriffs are not noted for their patience and Walter's long, and patently untrue, ramblings did not much please the bench who would have preferred to just get on with this open and shut case and move swiftly to the others in the queue. The tactics were wrong. Walter got three months and Dunky six. At least he tried.

There were some dramatic scenes at the Barlinnie gate when the three months were up. A jeep, with a corporal and three soldiers with rifles, arrived from Maryhill Barracks to escort Walter Norval back to Donnington. Pushed out the massive gates by the 'screws' he threw himself on to the ground and announced, 'I'm no' goin'.'

'You have got to go,' said the screws, by now beside themselves with laughter at the sight of their criminal charge seated, in the middle of the road, and refusing to move. The strong arm of the British Army had to come into play and Norval was dragged into the jeep and taken off to the Central Station. There the pantomime continued. He had to be dragged on to a mail cart and wheeled the length of Platform One to the train. For the watching commuters it was a sight they were unlikely to forget.

And nor would anyone at Donnington be likely to forget Walter's stay when he eventually got there. Not for nothing was he to write himself into the history of the camp and become known as the Mad Scotsman. This was a tough place but, although it was to become the scene of one of the bloodiest and nastiest episodes in Walter Norval's army life, it was no Alcatraz – escape was possible.

Hardly back in khaki, Walter was soon over the wall on the run again. This came about after he struck up a friendship with a character who had been a funfair worker in civvy street. This prisoner was known as 'Gypsy' Blundred and he was a fellow with all the nomadic urges of his kind. Blundred had noticed, in the paper, that a funfair, which he had once worked for, was visiting Wolverhampton which was around forty miles away. He suggested that Walter joined him on a visit to the fair. This seemed a good ploy to the restless Glaswegian and he devised a plan of escape.

One night, they went to bed fully dressed under the bedclothes and, in the morning when the corporal who had been tasked with guarding them was distracted, they clambered up over the barbed wire fences and legged it away across a couple of miles of fields. Incidentally, the corporal was one of the hapless victims ensnared in the mayhem that was life around Norval – he got twenty-eight days in the same army prison as his charge for his carelessness in letting the escape happen. It took Walter and his gypsy friend twelve hours to make it to Wolverhampton on foot. There were frequent stops to wipe blood from hands, legs and arms that had been torn by the mad scramble up and over the wire fences and their wounds had been made worse by having to struggle through clumps of thorns as they looked back over their shoulders anxiously searching for potential pursuers.

The funfair turned out to be less than fun for the Scot. Blundred had a comfortable pad in a caravan and Walter slept under a tarpaulin outside, fed occasionally with tea and toast from his new found travelling friends. And, as usual, the spell of freedom did not last long. The police raided the fair looking for deserters and 'Gypsy' Blundred was apprehend. Although he escaped the initial raid, it was not long before Walter, too, was nicked and back at Donnington – and he was soon to be in even deeper trouble than usual.

In civvy street and in the army he had a short fuse and this led to him getting into vicious fights with regularity. In these rages, he could wield his fists or a knife or a bottle without a thought of damage he could do. When the 'red mist' descended, he was a dangerous man. Down the years, there are many victims who can testify to the terrifying violence he could dish out. His victim, this time, was a sergeant who was much hated in the camp for his aggression, his loud-mouth, parade-ground shouting and all-round bullying of the young soldiers who were in his charge and at his mercy. This tinpot dictator in khaki made even more enemies when the national service men were in town enjoying a pint and the company of local girls. It was his habit to enter the pubs and hotels favoured by the squaddies and berate some luckless youngster about his deficiencies as soldier in front of his girlfriend and anyone else who happened to be in the pub. He was a nasty piece of work who had a comeuppance heading his way. It was to be bloody and violent.

Back in the camp one fateful day, he ordered Walter to get out of bed and fast. Told to fuck off, he persisted and Walter saw that red mist before his eyes. He leapt out of bed, punching and kicking his army superior in a mindless outburst of pure violence. In the ensuing rammy, the room got trashed and windows were broken. Walter used the shards of broken glass to slash his tormentor horribly. He also ripped up his mattress and then set it on fire with matches he had hidden in his uniform. If his actions had resulted in the camp burning down, he could not have cared less. The smouldering stuffing of the mattress produced thick clouds of choking smoke. Norval knew he would get a 'doing' when all this mayhem was over and he was determined not to give up without a memorable fight. He was in some form of blacked out rage. It took a squad of soldiers, led by a captain in the medical corps, to quell this one-man mutiny and, for their trouble, the soldiers were showered with broken glass which was thrown out, through the clouds of smoke from the burning mattresses, like missiles from a naval cruiser. Even the fearsome Alsatians of the military police couldn't scare him into submission.

But dragged out Norval eventually was – and with a certain degree of irony too since he, himself, had almost choked to death in the smoke produced by the burning mattress. Even more ironically, the first thing he was offered, presumably to calm him down, was a cigarette. Ambulances had been called and the next stop was a military hospital where a psychologist attempted to pin down the reason for such awesome aggression. Walter was still, even at this stage in his career, influenced by his old mentors in the Garscube Road, Foy and O'Hara. Both of them had 'worked their ticket' out of the army by a conscientious and planned operation of fighting and being difficult as possible at every opportunity. Walter had similar notions and was happy to feign madness in his efforts to get back to civilian life.

The efforts to assess his mental fitness had the occasional humorous side. The captain, who had led the efforts to end the berserk attacks that had put Norval and his victim in hospital, was convinced that his lonely and unloved childhood was at the root of his instability – not a bad diagnosis, I would say. But, true to the shrinks of that era, the captain conducted a few tests of his own on Walter. One was to offer him the clichéd round peg test. Given a board with some holes in it and a selection of pegs, round, square and triangular and asked to put the correct peg in the correct hole, Walter opted, somewhat obviously, for the square peg and round hole. After fiddling around for a bit and getting nowhere, he asked the good doctor for a hammer to help knock the peg in! Forget it, said the shrink in uniform, here is another little test. This time, he handed him a light switch which had been taken to bits and asked our hard man to put it back together. When the doctor wasn't looking, Walter hoisted a few of the parts through the window. Test failed – again.

Another ploy was to go on a hunger strike. The actual process of starving oneself is, according to Walter's memory, not as dramatic as it seems. Gradually, the torment of not eating is replaced by a kind of strange mental state in which the desire to eat has been overtaken by the desire to achieve a given end – in his case to convince the authorities that he was more trouble than he was worth and that he should be sent back to civilian life as soon as possible.

The army, however, met this sort of thing all too often and the response was force feeding. This has horrific connotations that go right back to the days of the suffragettes. But, in the army jails, in those days, it was not a big deal. Walter was pinioned, a tube was put down his throat and a life-sustaining fluid poured down it with all the finesse of someone pouring petrol into the tank of a car that has run out of fuel. After a few sessions of this undoubted cruel and inhume treatment, the hunger strike was called off. A body and mind honed into realism by years of institutional treatment had decided that enough was enough.

In the prison hospital, with the erstwhile King of the Twilight Zone back to eating whatever unappetising fare was put before him, the medical men turned to chemicals to calm the Mad Scotsman down. The pills probably weren't strong enough – what was? – and there were other violent episodes in the continuing attempt to work his ticket.

The prison shrink was still convinced that a lonely childhood had played a major role in turning Walter into the conscienceless violent and dangerous man he had become. He told Walter that he would move him into the big hut with other prisoners rather than keep him in solitary. The idea was that company would help him settle and ease some of the tensions and aggressions in him. 'Don't let me down, son,' was his plea and Walter agreed to his side of the bargain – but fate was to take a hand and the experiment was to end in disaster.

In the dorm he was sent to was a hapless young lad who was about to be moved from Donnington to do time in Colchester prison. He asked Walter what the infamous nick was really like. Walter drew on his vast experience of prison life and painted a mostly true picture of Colchester as a hellish place where the screws made life a misery for the inmates by constantly forcing them do their bidding at the double, often weighed down with heavy backpacks. The misery of the dank and dripping wet cell was spelled out in graphic detail. No smidgen of the miserable life was left unrecorded and it was all imprinted on an impressionable and fearful young mind.

It all made a mighty impression on the poor unfortunate waiting for his escort to transport him to such a hell in England's green and pleasant land. So much so that he hatched a plan to avoid the transfer that involved slashing his wrists with a razor blade which left his bed sheets dripping and crimson with his blood. He then hid the blade under the sleeping Norval's bed. So the Glaswegian, for once the innocent party, found himself being shaken awake in the dead of night by a captain and several privates and they were in no mood to believe his claims that, on this occasion, he was not involved.

So that was end of the experiment in allowing Walter to sleep in the dorm with the other prisoners. He was packed off back to solitary and only allowed out an hour a day to wage war on the caterpillars in the cabbage patch, his wild-eyed 'madness', as previously noted, watched by the locals passing along a nearby country road. The 'Mad Scotsman' was almost a tourist attraction. He stayed in solitary until his trial for the attack on the sergeant.

In the end, he did get out of uniform and the army finally gave up on mission impossible – the attempt to turn him into a clean-cut disciplined soldier. The Green Howards, you feel, had a lucky escape.

The bloody attack on the loud-mouth sergeant led to a full-scale court martial, a sentence of eighteen months hard labour in Shepton Mallet and an ignominious discharge. The only person who spoke up for Walter Norval at the court martial was the army shrink who plugged away at the effects of his lonely upbringing. However, he agreed that Norval undeniably did suffer from mental blackouts and had homicidal tendencies. The high-ranking officer – resplendent with his polished leather belt, glistening buttons and red sash – who presided over the case, had only one worry. Like anyone else who listens to the story of the Bad Soldier Norval, the presiding officer wondered aloud why it had taken the army so long to get rid of him.

For Walter Norval, well used to the hardest of prison regimes, the most important thing was that he was now on his way out of uniform. And he took particular satisfaction on a couple of points. He enjoyed the irony that his discharge papers informed him that, should he ever attempt to rejoin the armed forces or even the merchant navy, he would be liable to two years in prison. Rejoining the army was not one of Norval's priorities. Another source of satisfaction to him was the fact that he was discharged 'with ignominy' while his pal Dunky, who also failed as a soldier, was simply 'discharged' – such is the criminal mindset.

But, before his national service ended, there was the small matter of the time to be served in Shepton Mallet. It would be many months before Norval's footsteps would once again echo menacingly up and down the Garscube Road. And to the end he was a troublemaker. In 'The Mallet', by a curious coincidence Walter met up with his old friend from borstal and Glasgow, his best man John Harris who was also about to be kicked out of the army and had only a couple of weeks still to serve. And, after Harris left to go north, who should arrive but Dunky? Here was another survivor of the Glasgow mob who was also heading for a discharge for various pieces of in-uniform criminality and misbehaviour. The two old pals were sent to work in the cobbler's shop and spent much of their time planning a party back in Glasgow to celebrate their eventual freedom. Dunky – due for release a fortnight before Walter – was to be the prime organiser of this event.

Walter was reluctant to see Dunky leave so soon. He was enjoying his pal's company so he took action – a final piece of rebellion at army life. Somehow he talked Dunky into wearing a Canadian uniform that they had managed to get access to on his way out of the Mallet, as the prisoners called it. This uniform was an altered version of that worn by the British servicemen of the time, with wider buttons on the trousers and facings on the lapels and it was greenish in colour rather than khaki. Not surprisingly, Dunky, who, as we have already seen, was somewhat easily influenced by Walter, was stopped at the gate and charged by the prison company commander with defacing the king's uniform. This cost him a week's remission which was, of course, the Norval plan. He puts it this way, 'This meant Dunky was only going out a week before me rather than a fortnight. I would only miss my pal for a week. He wasn't pleased with me at the time but relented when I explained that I didn't want us parted for a whole fortnight before going home to Glasgow – after all, pals should stick together! He agreed.' No doubt that 'wee party' back in Glasgow was an epic.

Walter, Dunky and John Harris were a remarkable threesome. Only Walter now survives, both his pals having died in 2002 in another of those coincidences that punctuate Walter's life. Walter didn't go to either funeral, preferring to remember his old friends in crime as they were – 'my childhood pals who shared prison and borstal, and many adventures in the underworld, with me'.

Vodka, vermouth and cigarettes on a balcony in the Spanish sun. It is 1977, not long before the Godfather, Walter Norval, the Mr Big behind a series of armed robberies in Glasgow, was sent down for a fourteen-year stretch in the altogether grimmer surroundings of Peterhead. But, for the moment, it is a touch of the free-spending sweet life for Norval.

Eye-catching Jean McKinnon, Walter Norval's long-time mistress, had the looks and dress sense to turn heads on their trips to the sunshine of Tenerife, But, when the good life stopped, she stayed loyal to the gangster, writing to him every day of the more than ten years he spent in prison.

The businessman dad with collar, tie and waistcoat, the son, Walter, angelic in the sailor suit much favoured for formal photography in the thirties. Little hint of the violent life the young Norval was to lead after the early death of his commercial traveller father, Archie.

Just out of borstal, Walter poses with Ina on his marriage. On his right, his best man, also just out of borstal, is his lifelong friend John Harris. Criminals of a similar stripe, Harris and Norval grew up together, went to jail together and robbed and fought on the streets together.

Walter with his mother Eva. They had a complex relationship and, on one occasion, he even believed that she had turned him over to the police. She was not around much in the lonely early years that helped shape the Godfather and he disliked her relationship with the evil pimp Joe 'the Pole' Kotarba. But, towards the end of her life, after the death of Kotarba, mother and son eventually became closer.

McD

NORVAL

A newspaper photograph taken at the end of one of the most dramatic trials in Glasgow's criminal history. The XYY Gang, their faces and their names at last revealed to the public, make their way out of court to begin long sentences. The Godfather can still manage a smile despite the years of incarceration that lie ahead.

POLDING

'The Godfather's Daughter' was a tag the tabloids loved to use about the young and glamorous Rita Norval. It was a term she disliked intensely. Here, freed after accusations of threatening police officers were thrown out, she poses for the press and tells them that her father and her husband, both jailed, have been taken from her and now all she has left are her children.

© Walter Norval

Some called him the Capone of the Cowcaddens and Walter Norval took no offence at any comparison with the Chicago mobster. But here it is more Crosby than Capone as he compères the Christmas concert at Dungavel Prison in Lanarkshire. He sang and introduced the other acts so well that the governor, the famous Agnes Curran, said it was the prison's best concert!

© Robert Jeffrey

The Tower Ballroom building at the Round Toll, Glasgow, as it was in 2003, emasculated by the removal of part of the top of the tower. The dance hall was on the top floor and the snooker hall, where the 'Wee Mob' polished their skills with cue and ball and plotted much villainy, was on the first.

Freedom at last. Walter was picked up from Penninghame Prison near Newton Stewart by 'connections' driving a gold-plated Roller. The champagne flowed. Here Walter and his daughter Rita and a driver stop for a souvenir snap at the roadside. His spectacular exit from custody caused much comment of the 'Who says crime doesn't pay?' variety from the prison officers bemused by the goings on.

Walter Norval and his daughter Rita, who plays such a major role in his life, pose in their glad rags in the warmth of a starry Mediterranean night, enjoying holiday cruise. It is a long way from the old Garscube Road and the many prison fortresses that played host to the Godfather down the years.

7

7

THE WAR OF NORVAL'S EAR

You might have thought that army life, or at least life in an army prison, would have provided excitement enough for one lifetime. Not for Walter Norval. He had what is now called, in certain quarters, an attitude problem. In his case, the attitude was take what you can get, spend it as fast as you get it and plan some new scam to raise more cash. But, above all, his maxims were resist authority and fight anyone who gets in your way. His early career in crime had started to win him something he craved – the respect of his peers. And the authorities, too, had his number as a maverick – as a little tale, involving his old nemesis Detective Joe Beattie, demonstrates.

While Walter languished in the army jail at Shepton Mallet, plotting some new madness, his young wife Ina was taking a stroll along the Garscube Road with their youngest, just a baby, in the pram. And who should they bump into on the street but the great detective? 'How's Walter?' asked the cop. Assured he was safely under lock and key, he turned his attention to the baby who promptly stuck out his tongue at the inquiring detective. 'Takes after his father, I see!' said the cop with a cynical smile.

It was no surprise to anyone on either side of the law that, on his inglorious discharge, Walter was swiftly back at doing what the did best – thieving, scamming and generally making cash the easy way. And, of course, brawling with anyone brave enough to take him on. He was moving up a notch or two on the

7

criminal scale. Now that he was out of uniform, he and Ina were ensconced in the house in Garscube Road while his mother and Joe the Pole, the hated Kotarba, moved into one the flats she owned in Ashley Street in the Twilight Zone.

Throughout his criminal career, Walter recognised the advantage of inside information and had no compunction in paying good money for tip-offs that could lead to a profitable heist. In these post-war years, black markets in all sorts of goods still flourished. Whisky, in particular, was in short supply and the sale of stolen booze made big profits. Walter developed a string of contacts in whisky bonds and distilleries and among railwaymen who had access to shipments of booze. He had, of course, a network of pub owners and barmen who were anxious to get their hands on contraband liquor. Walter always like to think of himself as a Glasgow Al Capone and, indeed, there were similarities – not least of which were the love of good clothes, good booze and the ability to organise and rule gangs of heavies. Big Al, however, was, eventually, caught by the Feds and imprisoned for tax offences rather than his violence. Walter's incarcerations were for more dramatic offences than fiddling his tax! However, at this stage in his career, Walter, who would certainly have enjoyed and thrived in the prohibition era, was, like the Chicagoan legend before him, big in illegal booze operations. He remembers, 'I got orders for cases of whisky for my pubs. The drivers delivered the orders, I collected the cash and we split the money'.

The money was spent in some surprising ways. Walter bought a little hut at Seton Sands, near Portobello, on the outskirts of Edinburgh – not exactly the sort of pad you might expect him to enjoy. It was located at a place called Bruce's Camping Grounds. In the days before families, even those of limited income, routinely jetted off to Florida or the Costas of Spain, there were many such places dotted round Scotland where families enjoyed a break in simple wooden huts with basic equipment. A bit of sunshine, a stretch of sand for the kids to play on and a break from the grime and noise of the city were appealing to the honest Joes who toiled in shipyard or factory. For many a Glasgow family, a wee hut in the Trossachs was a cherished dream. Walter could have bought such a place there – it's only a few miles from the Garscube Road tenements to the shores of Loch Lomond and the Campsie Fells but, instead, for some reason, he chose the east coast and Seton Sands. Walter would spend the week in Glasgow, 'keeping things going' as he puts it, and then repaired to the camp grounds at the weekends to enjoy a bit of family life.

Always a keen gambler, he noticed a guy lifting betting lines at the gates of the camp. This illegal bookie was in the habit of paying out the winning lines at teatime after all the races had been run. Walter had a better idea – shuffle betting – and made a deal with the bookie to start paying out the punters after every race. This is, of course, long before the days of bookies' shops with direct phone lines from the tracks and the camp bookie couldn't get the results till the meetings were over. Mobile phones were a distant scientific dream and even having a phone in the house was something special. But, at almost every corner, there was one of the old red Post Office phone boxes. Luckily, there was one outside the Seton Sands camp site. So Walter arranged for friends in Glasgow to phone the results to this box after each race and this meant they could pay out the lucky punters there and then. And, of course, the punters could then invest their winnings right away on the next race giving the bookies more than a fair chance to get their money back. It worked a treat and the new partnership thrived.

Back in Glasgow, racing still featured large in the Norval way of life with excursions to the tracks round the Scottish central belt – like Lanark (now just a memory), Hamilton, Musselburgh, Ayr and others – in the company of Biadge Jaconelli and John 'The Bull' McCormack. Walter carried the cash, presumably to make sure it was in the safest, hardest hands. Big John was the clerk and 'B' took in the cash from the punters and paid out the winners. At the tracks, Walter would parade up and down in front of the other bookies studying their boards and keeping his connections in touch with what was happening. If a horse was being gambled on from, say, 10–1 with 'B' and Walter saw the price dropping to say 6–1 elsewhere, he promptly alerted his mates in case they got caught out. This racecourse activity was also helpful to the family as it brought in a regular income.

During this time, Walter also collected the rents from his mother's flats and, presumably, he encountered few problems with late payments – such was his reputation on the streets. He also made sure that the tenants created no trouble and generally smoothed out the operation. He was not the sort of man you picked an arguement with. It was far from a life of sweetness and light. When, years ago in borstal, Walter immediately assessed Joe the Pole as bad news, he was spot on. Kotarba was to bring all sorts of complications into the Norval family's life.

It began to get heavy with an early morning call one day summoning Walter down to his ma's flat. The police were hunting for Kotarba who had been, in Walter's words, 'messing about in Dennistoun with another Pole, Tony Kobuchia' who stayed in Thompson Street. A woman, Janet Davidson, was dead – murdered. Joe the Pole was in hiding and Walter's mother's flats were being turned upside down in the hunt for him – much to the concern of the lodgers who were just looking for a peaceful life. Janet Davidson was a prostitute and had been having a relationship with Kotarba behind Walter's ma's back. Joe the Pole, a notorious pimp and brothel keeper, was the number one suspect. Janet had a friend called May Boyle who was also a prostitute and who was staying with Kobuchia. She told the police that Kotarba had killed Janet in front of her and Kobuchia.

The police continued to turn over the flats searching for him and for clues and giving the many lodgers no peace. Walter

Norval decided to act. He contacted friends in the east coast and they found Joe Kotarba hiding in Musselburgh. Walter went through, confronted him and pointed out that he would have to talk to the police at some stage or his mother and her lodgers would be subjected to weeks of trouble from the law who were turning over the flats with fiendish enthusiasm. Walter brought him back to the Northern Police Office. They were interviewed by a detective called Neil Beaton who held Joe and, after couple of hours, Walter left. But Joe and Tony Kobuchia denied the only piece of evidence the police had, the statement by May Boyle, and the accusations didn't stick. Kotarba was released but the saga of Joe the Pole was far from over.

Despite this close shave, he had not been scared out of the pimping business. But, a couple of months later, Walter and his ma threw him out and he got a flat in West End Park Street and started running a brothel in it. Walter gave him a heavy message to keep away from his ma and her flats as he was now looking after that money-making little empire. But history was to repeat itself. Not many weeks later, a young woman was found dead in the West End Park Street flat. Once again, suspicion fell on the vice king, Joe, but he claimed the girl, Irene, had been killed by a punter in the brothel. Again he escaped justice. Years later, when he had been drinking, this evil man would threaten his prostitutes with the fate that had befallen Janet and Irene. This wicked boastfulness would eventually lead, indirectly, to his own death at the hands of Agnes Delacorti.

These years of the middle fifties will be remembered by Glasgow's criminal elite as the Carmont years. Carmont was a judge with a belief that the only way to curb gang crime and razor slashing in particular was to impose truly harsh sentences. It was effective and the slashers and would-be slashers took note. So much so that, as I tell in my book *Glasgow's Hard Men*, 'doing a "Carmont"' became street crook talk for serving a long stretch in one of Scotland's tough prisons. Lord Carmont was a judge of the Court of Session and the High Court of Justiciary for thirty-one years and he was at work right up to a fortnight before his death, on holiday in Kirkcudbright, at the age of eighty-five. By all accounts he was a gentle and kindly man but he was firm in his belief that the public deserved maximum protection from thugs and that the only way to provide this was to lock up criminals for long periods.

On one particular circuit, he passed sentences of up to ten years, and totalling fifty-two years of imprisonment, on eight people who had been convicted of crimes of violence. This circuit earned him praise in his *Glasgow Herald* obituary. In a lapse into tabloidese by that august newspaper, he was labelled as the man who 'rocked the underworld' and indeed he did. Walter Norval remembers well the speculation when the first Catholic slasher appeared before Lord Carmont who was a Catholic himself. The tabloids were also, in Walter's words, 'building up a big squeal' about what the judge would do when this happened. This first Catholic to appear in the dock to test the judge was Willie Collins, one of the High Road boys.

Just before Willie appeared, a gangster called John Totten had been handed down five years for using two razors in a fight that resulted in his victim receiving many stitches in one of the overworked emergency departments of Glasgow's hospitals. And another slasher was given seven years for slashing a man right across his face – an injury that, again, required many stitches. Willie Collins' offence was to cut an enemy on the cheek. It was a wound that required a modest two stitches and, for this, he got ten years – five years a stitch. The underworld got the message but it was not considered fair treatment. As Walter says, if the tariff had consistently been set at five years a stitch, some of the city's razor men would still be in jail to this day. But there is no argument that Carmont's reign did do much to curb the use of the razor or knife on Glasgow's streets. Walter had further first hand experience of justice Carmont-style when a former member of the Wee Mob appeared before this toughest of judges and he, too, went away for a ten-year spell.

Despite this, the malign influence of Kotarba and his friends was still being felt in the Twilight Zone. There had been a gruesome murder that the morning tabloids, ever eager for a new sensation to grab headlines, had labelled 'The Tricycle Killing'. And Walter played an unwanted role in it – thanks to his connection with Kotarba whom he hated with a deep intensity for his mistreatment of his mother and his suspicions that the Pole was stealing her money. Walter was in bed with his wife one morning when, at 7 a.m., there was a frantic knock at the front door of the Norval flat. Outside, in state of distress, was a man called Frank Gacic, a friend of Joe the Pole. Gacic asked Walter to take him to the police as he had just killed his girlfriend Margaret Doyle. Doyle was a prostitute and she lived with Gacic who pimped for her. Walter asked what had happened and was told that Gacic had beaten her up for spitting on him and kicking him in their flat in Hill Street. Walter asked if he was sure the girl was dead and couldn't he have phoned an ambulance or the police himself. 'She's dead!' was all Gacic could say.

Walter took him to the Northern where, by coincidence, the CID detective on duty was none other than Joe Beattie, now promoted and moved off his old beat on the High Road. Walter told Beattie that this guy Gacic had gone home and found his girlfriend dead. Beattie asked his old adversary what he knew about this and Walter said, 'Only what Gacic told me.' which was that he had come home from a night at the dancing and found Margaret dead.

Beattie took the house keys and went to the scene as Walter and Gacic sat it out in the bleak surroundings of the Northern. After a long two hours' wait, Beattie returned with other policemen, his face flushed with anger. He took one look at Gacic and snapped, shouting, 'Lock that bastard up.' He turned to Walter and said, 'You should see what state that flat is in. It's

103

splashed from roof to walls and floor with blood. He has smashed that girl to a pulp. Think yourself lucky that you never went up to see if she was still alive.' (In their initial interview with the police, Walter had mentioned that he had asked Gacic to take him up to the flat in case there was a chance that she was still alive and they could save her but the killer was adamant that the victim was dead.) For the blood-stained flat to have had such an effect on a detective of his experience, it must have been an almost incredible scene of horror.

Gacic got fifteen years for the bloody murder of the girl. He had battered her to a pulp, using the handlebars of a tricycle to smash her head in and slashing her body to ribbons with a six inch nail – hence the gruesome headlines. Although Gacic was sentenced to be caged for fifteen years, he was released after ten. Five years after his release, Gacic was back in his old routine. He was staying with another prostitute who, like his previous victim, was called Margaret. Like her predecessor, this Margaret, who was regularly mistreated, also snapped but, instead of spitting and kicking her tormentor, she killed him. Walter Norval's comment on Gacic's death? 'Coincidence or poetic justice, you name it!'

The killer got two years but Walter would have given her a medal for removing Gacic from the face of the earth. At the trial, much was made of his vicious behaviour to his girls. A few weeks before Gacic's sordid death, Walter got a visit from a friend who told him that there was a young woman in Kent Road, in a house owned by a Polish friend of Gacic, who was in a terrible state. Gacic had tortured her, beating her with a cane till she was covered in long weals, from her shoulders to her knees, on both the back and front of her body. Blood dripped from her to the floor. Gacic had taken her to the house after getting her drunk and whipped her to within an inch of her life.

Kotarba, too, treated the girls who worked for him with almost unimaginable torture using bottles and anything else that came to hand in sickeningly perverse behaviour. Walter went to that house in Kent Road and heard a story that shocked even him. It was a story that seems, to anyone not involved with crime or prostitution, to be almost beyond belief. Walter was told that Gacic was torturing and punishing a girl called Joan 'to prove he loved her and to impress on her that she was not to go with any other man without payment'. Walter told the Pole who owned the house that, while the girl was there, he was never to let Gacic into the house. He told him to give Gacic the message that, if he didn't stop, he was unlikely to be around long enough to hurt any other girls.

But, as it turned out, there was no need to take action because Margaret snapped and solved the problem herself. Gacic had been threatening her and her children and, during his final outburst, she had gone berserk and killed him. 'But what Margaret?' muses Walter as he recalls this horrific episode. Could the spirit of the original victim of Gacic, also called Margaret, have joined in his bloody downfall?

Both Kotarba and Gacic had, at one time, fought on the German side in the Second World War and Gacic claimed to have bombed London while in the Luftwaffe. He may well have been telling the truth for Kotarba confirmed that Gacic had been in the German Air Force. Even if they had wanted to return to Poland after the war, neither Kotarba or Gacic could have done so with any degree of safety. The Russians kept records of the Poles who had helped the Germans and these two evil men could not risk a return to their homeland. Kotarba, however, had kept in touch, by letter, with his mother, a peasant woman living in a rural area of Poland. He told her of his good fortune in marrying a widow with a bit of money and that his new wife had a son who was something of a name in the area. The old woman wrote back saying that he should 'beware of the widow's son'. Good advice.

Gacic was interred in an ancient graveyard near the old

Belvedere Hospital, off London Road in the city's East End. (Kotarba, who was also to end up being murdered, was buried in Lambhill cemetery.) Walter attended the evil pimp's funeral and, after Gacic had been safely covered by sod and earth, he and his connections held a party at the house of another middle European exile, a guy known as Benny the Pole. Much was drunk and many were the toasts to the death of Gacic. It was, says Walter, 'a celebration of the demise of a bad man.'

Around this time, Walter conducted an untypical experiment – he tried working for a living. He chose a hard living but the family had expanded and, as well as Ina and himself, there were now four other mouths to feed – Archie, Rita, Gerald and Lynn. So, it was a return to the Argyll countryside for Walter – the first time he had been back there since his adventures as an evacuee in Lochgoilhead. As part of the great post-war expansion of water-powered generating stations in Scotland, the Hydro-Electric Board were tunnelling in the hills at the Rest and Be Thankful, on the road to Inveraray. Walter had help in getting the job from an unlikely source – Kotarba and his Polish friends who were working on the hydro schemes – and, for once, he was toiling on the right side of the law to feed his family.

The Board had set up a huge temporary camp, called Butterbridge, for the tunnellers and the other ancillary workers involved in such a massive civil engineering project. Above or below ground, this was hard work – light years away from the sort of life Walter Norval had led up until then. He was employed as a clerk, working twelve-hour shifts, and, at the end of the shift, one of his duties was to measure how far the tunnellers had drilled into the rock each day. A small train ran on rails, through a narrow tunnel, right up to the rock face. It was used to take away the loose stones and rubble extracted by the tunnellers who were working in the noisy, sweaty darkness, deep in the hillside. In such a narrow tunnel, the little locomotive and its wagons posed an ever present danger for the unwary.

And, sure enough, that was to be the reason for Walter's short career as a legitimate worker coming to an end.

In a moment of carelessness, he was trapped, in a particularly narrow part of the tunnel, and the passing locomotive crushed him against the rock wall. In a horrendous journey over that bumpy mountain pass, the Rest and Be Thankful, he was taken in an ambulance to nearby Arrochar where a doctor administered morphine to ease the pain of his massive injuries. From Arrochar, on Loch Long, he was rushed by ambulance to the Western Infirmary in Glasgow for emergency surgery. His spleen had been split in two and had to be removed. The other injuries were so severe that he had barely enough blood left in him to keep him alive. The surgeon who saved him, Professor Fleming, reckoned he was within two hours of death.

It seems clear that working for a living was no longer attractive and Walter recalls that, from then on, 'honesty was the last thing on my mind'. He took four months to recuperate at his hut in Seton Sands. While he was there, his companion was a character from Baillieston on the outskirts of Glasgow, a pal called Bobby Francis, who did the cooking and massaged Walter back to health. His ongoing passion for keeping fit must have played a role in his recovery from injuries that would have killed or crippled many a man. During this period, Ina and the family came through to the hut from Glasgow for the weekends, returning in time to get the kids to school on Monday and, thus, showing more respect for the need for education than Walter did when he was a youngster. At Seton Sands, Walter played host to another face from the Glasgow street fighting scene – Colin Beattie who was known as Collie or simply The Big Man. Collie travelled from his patch in Partick to visit the recovering leader of the Wee Mob. And, with his wife and kids, he would spend a fortnight at the wee cabin on the east coast on occasion. Every district had its hard men in those days and Beattie 'ran' Partick for many years. He had a fearsome reputation as a fighter but he did have some social graces as well. He never tolerated swearing in front of women and, when he told someone breaking that rule to stop, they stopped. You didn't argue with The Big Man. Proof of his toughness comes from the assessment he received from Walter Norval – an assessment that must be the ultimate accolade. To Walter Norval, Collie, this giant of the streets, was the hardest man he had ever met!

On his return to Glasgow, and with any notion of an honest day's toil forever forgotten, Walter took over the running of his mother's flats, allowing her to retire. Rent collecting and dealing with property problems and demands of the lodgers wasn't enough to keep him out of other more productive and criminal ploys – like a bit of loan-sharking, working with the bookies and 'anything that brought in a bit of money'.

As a young Jack the Lad about Glasgow, Walter Norval was always something of ladies' man. Despite, or perhaps because of, his abilities with fist and knife and his fearsome reputation amongst fellow gangsters, he always attracted women and openly enjoyed their company. But he liked that company on a conventional one-to-one basis. However, he did once, just once, get involved in a three-in-the-bed situation – although it turned out to be pure bedroom farce rather than some erotic porn escapade.

Like a lot of episodes in a life of crime, drink was a factor. Walter's long-time associate Dunky White had remarried and had a new house in Barnes Road so a house-warming was in order. Walter remembers that 'there was a lot to drink' – something of an understatement, you might imagine. Another old pal, Johnny P, who had spent many a night on the rooftops with the Wee Mob, left at the death, as they say in Glasgow, with Walter and they hailed a taxi to take them home. Inside the black hack two thoughts collided. One – they didn't have any money for the fare – and two – Walter recognised the driver as a guy he had seen, not so long ago, roughing up an old fellow outside the Jungle Bar in the Cowcaddens.

Walter ordered the driver to take them to one of Joe the Pole's brothels in West End Park Street. There the fall-out, that was just waiting to happen, occurred – the driver 'copped a few wallops' and his passengers dived into the brothel. The taxi driver called the cops who arrived with some speed. There was only one lady of the night on the premises at the time and, on hearing the police, Walter and his mate decided to hide in a bedroom. They dived, fully clothed, into a bed – only to discover that it was occupied by what he remembers simply as 'a wee man'. The punter found himself unexpectedly caught up in some mayhem and he was told to keep quiet. He complied but the police still discovered the three of them in the bed.

The upshot was that Walter was charged with assault and sent for a sheriff and jury trial. The policeman, who gave evidence, made constant reference to the 'three-in-a-bed'. That famous old Scottish verdict, not proven, rescued Walter and Johnny was fined for Breach of the Peace. After it was all over, Johnny's wife, who had been in the court, remarked that he was lucky that the third party in the bed was a man, not a woman, or she might have dispensed some serious justice on her own part!

By now, it was the sixties and, although he was staying in the Garscube Road flat with his wife and kids, Walter was still a fighting man. Things were about to turn really nasty and bloody and trouble didn't always start in the pub or betting shop. Nor did there have to be a deep enmity or any long-lasting feud for it to erupt. Violence could spark out at any time and in the most surprising places. For some in Glasgow, fighting is truly a way of life and even a simple night spent entertaining friends could explode.

What you might call, if you had a historical turn of mind, the War of Norval's Ear was a case in point. Like many a war, it started on a somewhat lower key than it ended. One night in 1963, an associate, Big Willie White, and his wife Nan came up to visit the Norvals in the Garscube Road flat. They were a well-connected couple. Nan had been married to Tony Queen who was a famous Glasgow bookmaker and close friend of Jock Stein, the Celtic and Scotland football manager.

On this particular night, the Whites had a character called Big Mick Gibson in tow and he stayed on in the flat after the Whites had called it a night. Big Mick and Walter fell out, surprise, surprise, and ended up fighting in the back-court. Walter had his opponent on the ground and was on top of him, getting the better of it, when Mick struggled round, sank his teeth into Walter's left ear and bit a lump out of it. Before the neighbours, who had arrived after the battle had started, could separate them, Mick had a cut above one eye and another below the other eye. But separate them they eventually did and the skirmish was over – for the time being. Walter bears the scar on his ear to this day.

A month after that back-court brawl, Walter was in the Garscube Bar playing dominoes with his old mates Dunky and John Harris. Willie West, a Possil lad well known to Walter, burst in on the company and told Walter that Big Mick was in Fallon's pub, up the road, accompanied by three pals. 'Walter, they have big knives and they want to kill you,' West reported. In true Sir Francis Drake style, Walter finished his game of doms before arming himself with a blade and marching up the road to Fallon's to take on this East End Armada who had eyes on his territory – something he would not tolerate. On top of this, the memory of that disfiguring bite on the ear was fresh in his mind. And, above all, there was no way he was going to let Big Mick make a name for himself on the High Road which was Norval's own territory and, as such, was not up for any takeover.

Walter tells it like this, 'Dunky and John followed me up to Fallon's. I entered the pub and challenged the intruder. We fought and he lost. I left him in a bad state and had to go into hiding.' A 'bad state' is something of an understatement. Big

Mick's heart stopped in the ambulance on the way to hospital and he had to be resuscitated. According to Mick's brother-in-law, the intruder from the East End was stabbed eight times and left on the pub floor. Walter Norval then turned and challenged Mick's friends. Discretion took the place of valour and they declined the opportunity. Norval hid out in Townhead where, the next day, he had visitations from a number of friends – Pop McCausland (who had known Walter since he was in short trousers), Jimmy Lawrence, Johnny Phillips and Mick's brother-in-law, Blackie.

Blackie told Walter how close he was to facing a murder charge and that it had taken a five-hour operation to save Mick who was alive but barely so. There was no way out. Old Pop phoned Joe Beltrami, the legendary and colourful Glasgow lawyer known as the Great Defender and a major figure in the modern history of crime in Glasgow. During his long career, Joe Beltrami has been involved in some remarkable occurrences, both in courtrooms and out of them. At one time, he was the lawyer for Arthur Thompson who became Walter's successor as Godfather – at least, that was how he was perceived in the public eye. The Great Defender, who also fought to get Paddy Meehan his freedom and wrote extensively on crime in Glasgow, never agreed that Glasgow had a Godfather! However, holding this view set him at odds with most of the public, police and crime writers whose opinion was that the city most definitely did have a Godfather – and a very powerful one at that.

A 'meet' between the fugitive and the lawyer was arranged and Walter was set to surrender to the police at midnight on Sunday. Walter took a subway ride on Glasgow's tiny underground railway – now nicknamed the Clockwork Orange – to a station previously chosen and Joe Beltrami arrived, above ground, in grand style, in a huge white Mercedes, with a couple of newspaper crime reporters in tow. The scene at the police station was almost surreal with Walter demonstrating both his sense of humour and total lack of remorse or guilt for a truly horrific crime. A bunch of CID officers were in the Northern Police Office – which was now almost a second home to Walter – to greet the surrendering party. One of them said, 'Well, Walter, you have done it this time – this guy might not live the night.' He then went to ask formally, 'Have you anything to say?'

Walter looked round the assortment of grave faces staring at him in expectation. Then he leaned forward and said to one of them, 'You are a dead ringer for Gordon Smith who plays for Hibs and Scotland'.

The cops shook their heads in disbelief and one of them snapped, 'Lock him up.'

At the resultant court trial, in March 1964, Walter was charged with the attempted murder of Gibson. The trial took place in the Glasgow High Court, an imposing pile, opposite Glasgow Green, that was later to play an important role in the criminal life of Norval and his clan. He was defended by one of Scotland's most flamboyant and best remembered QCs, Nicholas Fairbairn. Nicky, who lived in a castle in Perthshire and was famous for his dandified dress, especially favouring tartan trews, had a controversial political life as a Tory and was a legendary drinker. He did a remarkable job of defending Walter and secured the relatively modest sentence of three years for a crime that came as close to murder as is possible. On form, Fairbairn was an impressive man to have in your corner. It is said that he defended seventeen people who faced the death penalty but never lost a client to the hangman.

There is a certain appropriateness in the fact that Fairbairn acted for Norval. As has been noted, it was perhaps watching Hollywood crime movies that inspired Walter to want to follow in the footsteps of Dillinger and his like. In a strange parallel, some say that seeing a film about the legendary US defence lawyer, Clarence Darrow, set Fairbairn on course to become a famous pleader. Dunky White also got three years for acting in concert with Walter. Much was made of mitigating circumstances. This was mainly owing to the fact that the wife of one of Gibson's friends gave evidence that she had heard her husband and Gibson, along with a mysterious third man who never featured in the trial, planning to kill Norval.

Walter was on his way to Peterhead and Big Mick never again ventured into his territory of the High Road. Walter now had the experience of being in Scotland's top security prison to add those garnered in such as Barlinnie, Saughton and the infamous Polmont Borstal. In his army days, he had also experienced the tough regimes of a selection of jails, including Shepton Mallet, the army's toughest prison. Shepton Mallet had been a civilian jail before the army took it over.

Something of an expert on the inside of prisons, Walter remembers Shepton Mallet as the place where they tried to hang an old villain called John Lee who entered criminal history as 'The Man They Couldn't Hang'. The story is told that they stood Lee on the trap and pulled the lever but the trapdoor would not open to let him through and thereby allow the rope do its work. After three failed attempts, it was decided that it was God's will that old Lee should not hang and, instead, he was given life. Walter inspected that famous trap door and the grim apparatus of the gallows which were still all in place when he was sent to the jail there.

This encyclopaedic knowledge of life behind bars had an amusing sequel for Walter.

In the fifties he heard a knock at his door one night. Outside was an emissary from the Bill Tennant's STV show asking if he would appear as an expert on prison life to discuss an outbreak of stabbings in the jails at that time. With his typical eye on the main chance, Walter only agreed after asking what was in it for him. The answer was a tenner a minute and that's what he got for a four minutes on camera spot. Tennant, at this time, was the top banana on STV current affairs. He was a podgy guy with a spotty face – rather different from the Pierce Brosnan types that are now employed to read the news and do interviews. However, he is well remembered and, in his day, he was very popular with his down-to-earth, matey style.

Walter was whisked to the studios and, during the warm-up and waiting period, he was seated beside a bearded healthy-looking outdoor type who was also waiting for his spot on the programme – presumably to discuss avalanches or mountain accidents or something of that sort. This rugged outdoorsman has his trusty backpack at his feet and, as Walter looked down at the backpack, he also suddenly noticed that his own shoes had dog poo on them – copious amounts of it. What to do? The fast thinker gave his shoes, the uppers highly polished as ever, a secret scrape on the nearby backpack belonging to the unsuspecting outdoorsman and was then called into the studio.

The show's host began with a preamble outlining for the viewers how valuable Walter's knowledge was because few people had been in so many prison establishments and nor had they spent so long behind bars. The rotund, ruddy-faced Tennant then postulated that the increase in the number of stabbings in prisons was all down to fights over 'snout' and that the tobacco barons, who play such a major role in prisons, were to blame. 'Rubbish!' said the bold Walter and he backed this up by saying that there was no way the tobacco barons would want their punters stabbing each other. He explained that, if you can't pay in cash or favours, you are off the list – simple as that. According to Walter, the real reason for the outbreak of stabbings inside jails was the preponderance of feuds which could either be recent or could have been festering away perhaps for years. His view was that, when a con heard that an old enemy was coming his way, he would have time on his hands to find, make or secrete a weapon but the new boy wouldn't have this luxury and, on his arrival in prison, the old score would be settled dramatically and bloodily.

His piece said, Walter left the studio and headed for the Garscube Road pubs. On his way out, he caught a glimpse of the next interviewee – the outdoorsman – on camera, complete with haversack, in full verbal flight and he wonders to this day if anyone knew where the pong was coming from. Back in the pub, his mates praised his performance and he won a smidgen more respect as gangster and TV pundit.

This touch of humour offers an insight into Walter Norval's sense of fun – a trait that even infected, on occasion, his successor as Glasgow's Godfather, the infamous and much feared Arthur Thompson. Thompson provided some light relief during one of Walter's sojourns in Barlinnie. One of their fellow inmates was a hard man with an Achilles heel. This gangster could hold his own with the 'chib' and blade merchants of the slums – spilled blood was no problem for him – and could coolly look down the barrel of gun but he was terrified of rats – and he was sure there were plenty in the Bar-L. (Actually, despite the appalling conditions the prisoners endured, rats were not a big problem.) In those days, inmates slept on mattresses placed on wooden platforms that were just a few inches above the floor. Had there been rats, of the four-legged kind around, this was just the right place for them to take a nibble at human flesh.

Aware of this man's morbid fear of the rodents, Arthur Thompson spotted a chance for a bit of fun. One day, a bit of an old scrubbing brush was found. With a length of cord attached to it, the brush was inserted into a pipe near the cell of the rat hater. A careful tug or two of the cord would produce a nice little scratching sound that had the victim jumping on to the table in his cell and screaming blue murder for the warders to rescue him from the rats that were clearly trying to break-in and make a meal of him. It provided splendid entertainment for his hard-hearted fellow inmates and passed a bit of time!

Another less than bleak memory of the Bar-L days occurs in musical form – a little ditty called 'Barlinnie Hotel'. In pubs and clubs, Walter Norval, along with his dad, used to sing the song about the death of the Celtic goalie, John Thomson. He has always enjoyed a sing-song and, when in mellow mood, he can give an intriguing version of this Bar-L song. As is the case with the 'Borstal Song', who wrote this and when is something of a mystery – certainly Norval can't tell you – but the words ring true with the thousands of Glaswegians, young and old, who ended up doing a spell in the . . .

BARLINNIE HOTEL

In Glasgow's fair city,
There's flashy hotels.
They give board and lodgings,
To all the big swells.
But the greatest of all now,
Is still in full swing,

Five beautiful mansions,
Controlled by the King.
There's bars on the windows,
And bells on the door.
Dirty big guard beds,
Attached to the floor.
I know 'cause I've been there,
And sure I can tell,
There's no place on earth like
Barlinnie Hotel.
I was driven from the Sheriff,
And driven by bus.
Drove through the streets,
With a terrible fuss.
Drove through the streets,
Like a gangster at state,
And they never slowed up,

116

Till they got to the gate.
As we entered reception,
They asked me my name,
And asked my address,
And the reason I came.
As I answered these questions,
A screw rang the bell.
It was time for my bath,
In Barlinnie Hotel.
After my bath, I was dressed like a doll.
The screw said, 'Quick march,
Right into E-hall.'
As I entered my flowery,[1]
I looked round in vain,
To think that three years here,
I had to remain.
For breakfast next morning, I asked for an egg.
The screw must have thought,
I was pulling his leg,
For, when he recovered, he let out a yell,
'Jailbirds don't lay eggs,
In the Barlinnie Hotel!'
The day came for me,
When I had to depart,
I was as sick as a dog.
With joy in my heart,
For the comfort was good,
And the service was swell,
But I'll never return,
To Barlinnie Hotel.

Sadly, Walter Norval and many like him, who may have sung these poignant words, too often returned regularly to the delights of Glasgow's famous old prison.

---

[1] Slang for cell.

8

Playing Ball in Peterhead

On his way to Peterhead, after being sentenced for the attack on Mick Gibson, Walter Norval had a meeting with an old friend who had influenced him significantly in his life of crime. Samuel 'Dandy' McKay was a legendary Glasgow bank-robber. He was a man with the rare ability to get his hands on the hard-earned cash of others and he also had a talent for spending it fast and spectacularly. He had that holy grail of the criminal community – respect – in spades. He, like Walter and as his nickname indicated, enjoyed dressing smartly. He could look after himself but was not, basically, a man of violence. And, on occasion, he could even feel the pang of social conscience – an example being when he was helpful to the police in the conviction of mass murderer Peter Manuel.

Manuel had tried to blame McKay for some of his actions but the police, who knew McKay well, would have none of it and, indeed, Dandy was so horrified by the killings that he did everything in his power to help bring the killer to court and, from there, to the Barlinnie gallows. McKay knew a lot about Manuel and was prepared to tell the police about most of it, complete with dates and times. This information helped enrich the case against Manuel and eventually he began to crack. There is no doubt that Dandy McKay played a significant role in bringing Scotland's most infamous serial killer to justice.

On Norval's long drive north from Glasgow, the prison bus, filled with the sweepings of the Glasgow courts, stopped at

Craiginches Prison in Aberdeen to feed and water the prisoners. A knock on the bus window attracted Walter to his old friend Dandy who, surprisingly, had a ladder under his arm – not what you'd expect to see when the prisoner concerned is so well known as a desperate man. But, by now, McKay was no desperate escaper ready to leap the wall to freedom. Dandy was in the final stages of a thirteen- year sentence for one of Glasgow's most famous criminal events – the Shettleston bank robbery. This had also resulted in the conviction of his associate – a gentleman known as the Monacled Major.

Dandy inquired if Walter was set for a spell in Craiginches but was told that, after they had been fed, he was bound for the altogether tougher regime of Peterhead. It was to be the last time they would meet but Walter still remembers the sage advice given to him by the old bank robber who told him, 'You are either a friend or you are not. You can't be half a friend'. Walter quotes this adage at every opportunity – doing a long stretch behind bars often turns a prisoner into something of an amateur philosopher.

Peterhead is the toughest prison pad in Scotland. When it was built, it was sited near a quarry and the stone the prisoners carved out of this quarry was used to build a breakwater for the local harbour. In the heyday of the quarry, guards, armed with .303 rifles, stood over the men and any attempt to escape led to shots being fired and, on one occasion, a prisoner was killed. In this instance, it was said that the officers fired to wound but that the bullet had ricocheted off the stone. Aye, right! When Walter arrived, the quarry had closed and some of the other trappings of Peterhead prison life were a memory – like the sabres carried on thick belts round the warders' waists. And the cat-o-nine-tales used as punishment for even minor offences against prison discipline and the practice of chaining and shackling of prisoners. Despite the fact that such things were no longer used, it was still a tough place and there were allegations that 'batter squads' of violent prison officers were still allowed to run free and dispense their own version of prison discipline with boot and club.

Walter, while unhappy about losing his freedom yet again, found his mental pain eased somewhat by what he describes as 'the realisation that I had reached the top prison in Scotland and was mixing with the top villains.' This curious justification of events, however, was founded on the notion that eventually, after release, and back on the streets, indulging in theft and violence, his status as an ex-Peterhead con would confer on him something that he longed for with a deep passion – that old ambition, respect.

Dandy wasn't the only old pal he was to meet on this stretch of prison time. Peterhead, with its grim walls, is an old prison, in the far north east of Scotland. When Walter was there, it was a damp and bleak establishment that was swept by powerful, cold winds, whipping off the North Sea and howling, like demented wolves, round the chimney pots and through the exercise yard. His time in borstal had provided Walter with a rare mixture of villainous friends who had, to a man, not been steered away from a life of crime by that violent regime. His old borstal mates turned up time after time to join him in both army and civilian jails, giving proof positive that any hopes of borstal successfully reforming its young thieves and thugs were doomed. They represented a failed dream of a society that did not truly understand the forces that drove such young men.

And this pattern of meeting up with those the borstal system had failed to turn away from lives of criminality was to be repeated again in Peterhead. Almost the first fellow prisoner Walter ran into was one Joe 'The Meek' Meechan who had done time with him in Polmont Borstal. An early conversation with Joe, at the start of his stretch in PH, as the prisoners call Peterhead, gave Walter an insight into how prisoners, institutionalised by long spells behind bars, could remember happenings of years ago as if they had taken place, as the saying goes, yesterday. Joe made a cup of tea and gave Walter the low-down on the lay-out and inmates of the jail.

And, over that cup of tea, a trivial matter was recalled. All those years ago, as he left borstal, Walter had given Joe a jacket which Walter describes as 'one of the tailor-made ones, hard to get and only made for the guys who had earned respect'. It was an act of generosity that Walter had long since forgotten but it was fresh in the memory of an old lag who had time on his hands to reflect on the past in the sort of depth that someone going about his or her business on the 'outside' just didn't have. This suspension of time is a curious and much remarked on effect of long spells in prison. The disruption of normal timescales has a powerful effect on the mind of the long-term prisoner. The sameness of each grindingly boring day means that little incidents are etched on the memory in a way that doesn't happen on the outside. Whatever else the prison regime had done to Joe it hadn't totally destroyed his sense of humour. He liked to entertain his fellow cons with boasts that, on release, he would be the richest man in the world. The justification of this unlikely belief came directly from one of the best read books in the prison – the Bible. It was there in black and white, claimed Joe Meechan for he had just read that Jesus had decreed that the meek shall inherit the earth.

From early on, Walter, as has been noted, was a faithful fan of his beloved Celtic but he was also an excellent footballer and, when not involved in 'tanning' warehouses or pubs, fighting bloody battles in the streets or flitting across the roofs tops of the city in the dark, he could be found on the football field showing the sort of form that could have got him on to the professional ladder and perhaps into a profitable life away from crime and violence. But the sort of life he led made regular training sessions and long spells in the same place impossible. Even as a boy, when he played for church teams, he was a 'ringer' – someone brought in, under a false name, to stiffen this or that side.

But the skills, fitness and determination were there. The nearest he got to pro-football was a spell with Bridgeton Waverley, one of the many junior teams that peppered Glasgow and its surrounding areas. Junior football was, and is, a rough old game with most of the teams fielding a mixture of ambitious young guys and failed professionals. The younger ones were fresh from amateur teams and would be ready to kick their grannies off the park for the promise of a fiver in their boots after the game. The failed pros were there to earn a last bob or two as their careers drifted into obscurity. Such teams had fanatical followings which, although tiny compared to the fan bases following the top league teams, could, at times, be just as passionately committed to their teams as any Old Firm supporter.

This was a world of hard drinking and hard, hard football with little emphasis on elegance or tactics and every emphasis on violent high-speed aggressive football. In short, it was a world where a man like Walter Norval, who had the natural football skills married to the necessary aggression and fitness, fitted perfectly. If only he had devoted more time to it, Scotland might have had another star of the football field and much villainy would also have been avoided. As it is, he now remembers his time in junior football as a pleasant interlude in a life of crime. When he watches Celtic, he often does so from the luxury of a celebrity box, mixing with the great and the good in the city who follow the fortunes of The Hoops. And the comments that he makes on what the sees on the field are informed by a deep knowledge of the game of football.

In Peterhead, during that first long stretch for the attempted murder of Mick Gibson, football played a major role in passing the time, keeping him fit and providing some achievements and 'goals' in life throughout those years of dreary monotony. The prison had a team and naturally Walter became one of its stalwarts. They were allowed to play teams from the outside. The north east was a stronghold of football at the junior level.

Only Aberdeen FC played in the top division. There were several Highland league clubs but difficult transport in the area and the large distances involved meant that football at the junior level was particularly well supported. The prisoners of Peterhead were allowed to test their skills against such famous junior and minor league teams as Sunnybank, Banks o' Dee, Buckie Thistle and Peterhead itself. These were teams that could find themselves at the old Hampden Park in Glasgow playing in the one game that all the juniors desired more than any other – the Junior Cup Final, a national competition that pitted junior sides from all parts of Scotland against each other.

Some of those north-east teams were semi-pro but, of course, the prisoners only played for the love of the game and a break in the regime. However, both sides took the football extremely seriously and, remarkably, during the whole time Walter was at Peterhead in his first long stretch 'up north', the prisoners never lost a game. But it was not a one man show. The prisoners' team had a fair sprinkling of ex-professionals, who had fallen on hard times, and they were no push over. The local RAF station, too, sent round a team but the fit young service men were, like the junior teams, sent away mourning a defeat by a bunch of highly motivated cons.

When nothing else was happening, the fortunes of the prison team became important to the hard cases incarcerated in PH. Some of the prisoners were not of the class to get into the top prison team. Walter remembers that Johnny Ramensky, the famous safe-blower who spent a life behind bars, was one such wannabe who never made it on the football field. Gentle Johnny, as he had been dubbed, was relegated to play in prison matches known as 'The Hams v. The Bams'. Football was such a part of prison life that they even had a shield to be played for by the various halls. 'A' hall boasted the largest number of inmates, 'B' hall had the smallest and there was also a team from 'C' hall. The halls played each other four times a season and, at the end, the winners were awarded the shield. In Walter's time his hall, 'B', were the winners.

Walter got on well with Ramensky who got his nickname from his habit of going quietly when collared by the police and always pleading guilty if he was guilty and, unlike Norval, eschewing violence. The Peterhead cons respected Ramensky for his legendary skill as a single-minded safe-blower with incredible skills, a man who concentrated on this one form of crime. They also admired him for his war-time exploits when he was dropped by parachute behind enemy lines to blow open safes for the allies in search of secret papers and German military plans. His training for this dangerous behind-the-lines work was meticulous – the military even procured a number of safes for him to practise on so that this legendary peterman could make sure he was in top form before taking a flight on a moonless night across war-torn Europe heading for a desperate and dangerous adventure.

Ramensky was another ex-Polmont Borstal boy who had suffered under the cruel boot-and-baton regime of the warders of that sad institution. His way of releasing the pressure of his frequent prison sentences was, where possible, to torture his body in the gym. He developed a lifelong passion for keeping himself fit. But, despite his fitness, his footballing skills were lacking – although he still loved to kick a ball about at every opportunity. However, in the opinion of Walter Norval and the other cons who formed the prison committee for football, poor old Johnny was nowhere good enough for the prison team – not only that, he was deemed to be not even good enough to play for his hall team! On Sundays, all the guys who, like Johnny, were the second- or third-raters on the football field, would get a game to suit their abilities. The football committee would pick two teams of the not-so-good to play each other in the amusingly named Hams v. Bams games – 'no disrespect, just a name picked for a laugh,' says Norval.

Gentle Johnny Ramensky (who had spent the majority of his

years behind bars died in Perth Prison aged sixty-seven) was always first to get his name down on list of those wanting a game on a Sunday. Ramensky is also well remembered, in the penal community, as a man who had been involved in major prison reform in Scotland in the thirties. One attempt at escape led to him being slapped in iron shackles in Peterhead and the public revelation that such inhumane practices, especially used on a man like Ramensky who abhorred violence, were still in use led to the then Secretary of State conducting a review of prison practice. The barbaric use of shackling was abandoned after this incident. The sadness of Johnny Ramensky's remarkable life is that, even after his valuable war service, he was unable to settle down to a life without the excitement of crime. Perhaps, in that way at least, he was similar to his fellow prison footballer Walter Norval – even if he was unable to match Norval's exploits on the field – I tell the full story of this remarkable man in *Gentle Johnny Ramensky* (Black & White Publishing, Edinburgh, 2010).

Ramensky was not the only crime legend held in Peterhead at that time. Some of the other inmates were of a more dangerous ilk than that of the safe-blower who forswore violence. There were men like John Gordon, one of Scotland's most infamous murderers who had grabbed the headlines in the famous 'McFlannel Murder'. *The McFlannels* was a hugely popular Scottish radio programme that featured a fictional family who lived up a Glasgow close. Listening to it was a Saturday night must for almost every family in the city. Now largely forgotten, it was an early radio soap opera whose weekly twists and turns spawned conversation over canteen tables in shipyards and factories, in pubs and on the buses and trams. In its heyday, everyone who had a radio seemed to have, at one time or another, listened to it. On that first spell in Peterhead, John Gordon, who had killed one of the cast, George McNeill who played 'Mr McZepher', was something of a celebrity convict among the wretched men who filled the cells, many of whom had made big headlines for all the wrong reasons. McNeill had been a lay preacher and Fairfield shipyard welfare executive as well as being a part-time actor. Big John Gordon had fled Govan to Barcelona, having attempted to join both the French and the Spanish Foreign Legions, and from there he was extradited back to Scotland to stand trial.

Years later, when Norval was back banged up in Peterhead, because of his exploits with the XYY Gang, John Gordon became a remarkable talking-point in the jail. One Sunday, one of the prison officers appeared with a story torn from that day's *News of the World*. The ever vigilant '*News of the Screws*', as it is known in newspaper circles, had uncovered a dastardly piece of news. An ex-lifer was exposed as one of the security group guarding Princess Anne – and he was none other than big John Gordon. Security around the royal family was far from efficient back then and this would still occasionally appear to be the case.

Gordon was, of course, a big-time criminal who spawned big headlines to match the size of his reputation but, in Peterhead in the sixties, there were many lesser lights who were also well known to Walter from his days in borstal – Alex McRobbie, John Burnside and John Swandles, among others. But Walter also made a new friend – and again he was a big-headline criminal. This was Donald Forbes who became the first man in Scotland to do two life sentences in a row.

Forbes and Norval struck up a close relationship and Walter still tells anyone who will listen that it is his belief that the double murderer was wrongly painted as an evil man by the tabloid press. Caged in Peterhead, Walter thought Forbes was a man whose only crime was 'to be in the wrong place at the wrong time'. This is not an opinion his victims would endorse and it is seen as a banal, even clichéd, excuse that many a villain down the years has made. Forbes had been sentenced to hang for his first killing but had been reprieved at the last minute. His second murder was said to have occurred when he was in a fight defending a drunk who was being beaten up by a crowd. Horrific as it all was, in the intimacy of prison life, Norval found a friend in Forbes.

As has been pointed out before, few men, in annals of British crime, have a longer and more varied experience of incarceration and its effects than Walter Norval. Yet he can talk of life in Peterhead as 'an experience. A world within four walls. A world full of villains and rascals but we were like a big family, full of guys with a great sense of humour and mostly family men with very good morals. Of course, there were fall-outs with some guys.' It is a view of prison life that might surprise the reformers and, indeed, the staff of the prison service – not to mention anyone who has no experience of the penal system – but it's a view worthy of some analysis. The layman may not like it but that is the verdict of the man who did the time.

Another person who became a great friend of Norval in prison was Willie Leitch. This man goes down in Scottish prison history as 'The Saughton Harrier', a nickname bestowed on him after one of Scotland's most remarkable prison escapes – an escape worthy of a featuring in a Norman Wisdom comedy film. Willie was working in the governor's garden at Saughton Prison in Edinburgh on the day that a marathon road race was due to pass by. With admirable quick thinking, he painted a number on his vest, simply jumped the garden fence and trotted to freedom, safe in the body of the race runners who all looked much like each other, wearing white vests with numbers on them. Years later, this escapade had an interesting sequel when Willie and Walter were in Dungavel prison near Strathaven in Lanarkshire. One day, a new governor arrived and sought them out in 'the sheds' where they were having tea. This governor turned out to be the one whose flower beds Willie had been tending when he jumped the fence to freedom. The governor lost no time in ticking Willie off and reminded him that, all those years ago when Willie had run out to join the race, the escapee had trampled all over the governor's favourite rose bed.

Willie Leitch, like Ramensky, had a dramatic spell in the services, in his case on HMS *Consort*. And for many years he has campaigned energetically for more recognition for the part played by the crew of HMS *Concord* who had also served in the far east. Willie feels strongly that political machinations involving Britain and China denied his fellow navy men a fair share of campaign awards.

However, no matter how hard people like Walter Norval tried to keep positive and seek out the humour in the prison life, all was not sweetness and light in the Peterhead of the sixties. Hardly a day went by without fights between cons and these often involved weapons that had been secretly manufactured by the prisoners and hidden away until an opportunity to use them arose. As well as fights between cons, there were the inevitable assaults on the screws. And, to make matters worse, rooftop protests and riots were making headlines galore. The tendency of Peterhead to epitomise the rougher side of prison life continued right into the eighties.

This was the time when one of the central figures in the Glasgow ice-cream wars saga, T C Campbell, was seldom out of the papers. There were stories upon stories outlining incidents in the prison involving him. His anger was fuelled by his aggressive belief in his innocence and, in his one-man war against the authorities in this high security prison, he had both victories and defeats. He was cleared when the prison regime took him to court and charged him with assaulting a screw or prison officer as they prefer to be called these days – the term warder is no longer considered politically correct. But a charge that he had been beaten up and kicked by a squad of prison officers in retribution for his part in one of many riots was thrown out.

One of his victories, and one with a resonance for many prisoners, was a planned action in the European Court of Human Rights in connection with alleged interference with his mail and other infringements. He also won damages of £250 in compensation for an attack of bed bugs that the authorities were regarded as having caused him to suffer. But his most memorable victory was to win an award of £4,000 in damages against the then Secretary of State for Scotland, Malcolm Rifkind. Campbell had claimed £40,000 but a civil jury made the lower award. They said that they were satisfied that injuries sustained by Campbell had been inflicted during the 'wrongful actions of prison officers'. It is often said that the best policy when in prison is to opt for the quiet life and keep your head down. Tackling the system head on is not to be advised. But T C Campbell proved that, on occasion, you can 'take on City Hall' and win.

His final vindication came in the spring of 2004 when his third appeal resulted in the guilty verdicts handed down on him and Joseph Steele in the Ice Cream Wars trial being overturned.

Campbell and Steele had spent twenty years in jail for a crime they did not commit. Their long incarceration was one of the most appalling miscarriages of justice in Scotland's history.

Another famous Peterhead inmate was Larry Winters. Norval met him in this first Peterhead term and he tried to impart some of his knowledge of how to handle prison life, garnered in countless nicks, to young Winters who had just been shipped up from Glasgow. In many chats, Walter told Winters that, if he could only keep out of trouble, he 'would be out in about eight or nine years' – as if that was just short time away! He ended up being sent back south, having been labelled a celebrity trouble-maker in that remarkable experiment of prison reform, the Barlinnie Special Unit. In the Unit, specialists had evaluated Winters as an extremely clever man – indeed, he was reported to have an IQ of 160. However, this high intelligence was accom-panied by low self-control – a potent and dangerous mixture. Walter Norval had spotted this weakness in Peterhead. He remembers Winters' refusal to take good advice and delivers a verdict that Winters had 'spent about thirteen years of his young life fighting a system that eventually destroyed him'.

In 1977, Winters' and Norval's lives touched again briefly when the Godfather was on yet another of his stays in Barlinnie. Walter was in C Hall for untried prisoners and Winters was in the Special Unit. A screw knocked on the door of Walter's cell to break the news that one of his 'old friends has been found dead in the Unit'. Winters was discovered naked on a chamber pot and had died of a drug overdose. Misuse of drugs in the pioneering Special Unit had always been a source of controversy and, in the end, such allegations had a lot to do with the closure of the Unit. This came about despite several undoubted successes in rehabilitating killers that most of society wanted to lock up and throw away the key. Like the many specialists in the Unit who tried to help Winters, especially by seeking to develop Winters' talent for writing, Walter found the young killer to be likeable. According to Norval, 'He died needlessly. He just turned the wrong way and fought a system that never loses.'

Peterhead, in the sixties, was full of Scotland's most notorious criminals. It boasted a role call of infamy that included Walter Scott Ellis, Banjo Ross, John McCann (known as the Aga Khan on the streets of Glasgow where nicknames are popular), Big John Currie from Motherwell, the bookie George Drummond and, of course, the Saughton Harrier. The cells, Walter said, contained 'every kind of rascal, including myself'. To a career criminal like Norval, engaged in every kind of scam and violence since he was in short trousers, these were 'all guys with good morals'. His definition of morality is a little out of kilter with that of society as a whole but he adds an interesting aside – no 'beasts', as cons call child molesters, came anywhere near the group he is talking about.

It would seem that being in prison breeds the same sort of closeness that sometimes develops between other groups who are forced to live together – in boarding schools or in the services, for example. Shared deprivation seems to bring about a compatibility among certain types of men. Walter puts it like this, 'We had all been through the system from our early days and understood each other.' By understanding each other, he means having the ability to adhere to their own idea of a criminal code. With Walter Norval, such a code has been an important part of his long criminal life.

It would be easy to be cynical about it but part of that code involves a fiver or two of his ill-gotten gains going in the direction of the old wifies in need of a bob or two or ensuring a spot of cash made its way to some pensioner, in a dark corner of a pub, slowly sipping a pint to make it last. Even in his days as an illegal money lender, Norval usually didn't take the going interest rate which was, on occasion, around 50% – often, if he lent someone a fiver, there would be a quid due in interest, with two quid for a tenner, four quid for twenty and so on. This was a horrific rate of interest but it was by no means the worst rate available on the block. But, like all money lenders, there would be no reluctance to take action if a debt was not repaid by a due date. If you didn't pay up, you risked your health and well-being – interest could be, and often was, paid in blood. Glasgow money lenders had muscle and no scruples about violently enforcing a pay back.

Prison was, as we have seen a place where old acquaintance-ships were revisited and new friends were made. In Peterhead, Walter met another young man who was to play a pivotal role in his career as a big-time armed robber. This young man would eventually to go down for twenty-one years as a result of getting involved in one of Norval's bank raids. He was John McDuff who was, somewhat unimaginatively, given the nickname of 'Plum'. He joined the Norval 'family' on his release, often staying in the family home and going everywhere with the man who was to become the city's first Godfather. Every general needs good lieutenants and, in the carefully planned and successful robberies that were to come, Plum was to become one of Norval's much-valued right-hand men. And he was to be a major feature in the long and acrimonious High Court trial that ended with Walter being put away for more than fourteen years and his gang being cut down by swingeing sentences. But, in the sixties, Plum was just one of the Glasgow criminal entourage that filled the cells in Peterhead.

Another was Bobby Campbell, father of T C Campbell who, along with Joe Steele, was at the centre of the ice-cream wars allegations. Incidentally, it is striking that Glasgow has produced so many criminal dynasties – notably, the Thompsons and the Ferrises, but there are others. Again, the reasons for this are often tied in with the nature versus nurture debate so beloved by criminologists, both amateur and professional. Certainly, some criminal genes seem to be running wild in the less salubrious areas of the city on the banks of the Clyde.

There would be many wealthy crime-writers around if they all received a tenner each time they heard a tale of wrongful imprisonment. However, some, who assert their innocence, have stronger claims than others and one of them is Bobby Campbell – at least as far as a particular ten-year stretch in Peterhead is concerned. Walter tells of how he was entertaining Bobby, over a cup of tea, in his cell, one night, when in walked the man who had committed the crime that had resulted in Bobby being shipped north. This bloke was serving five years in Peterhead for an unconnected crime. The three of them sat looking at each other and sipping their tea. Bobby Campbell remarked, with a laugh in his voice, 'I'm doing a ten stretch for you.'

The other con, far from fazed, simply shrugged his shoulders and remarked, 'Well, Bobby, that's the way the cookie crumbles.'

Norval, too, was philosophical about this turn of events. Now, years later and after many other episodes of crime and punishment have passed, he can say, 'It was all said in good humour and accepted the way all cons accept that you don't grass – even if you know who has committed the crime you are being blamed for. These were the rules we lived by. Bobby was a man of respect.' The strength of the criminal code cannot be underestimated but, in today's world of drug dealing and people trafficking, you would have to wonder whether such simplistic rules would still apply. I suspect not. But, in the sixties, it was still possible to think such thoughts.

Walter paints an intriguing picture of life behind the high walls of Peterhead. In the evenings, the cons spent much time watching TV or playing cards. There was a hot plate at one end of each landing in the various halls and a TV at the other. Those unimpressed by the TV scheduling for the night would play cards round the hot plate before spending the long hours of the dark night in the loneliness of their cells. During the day, all the cons were assigned to work parties. There was a tailor's shop, a joiner's and a mattress maker's, among others. These workplaces were all contained in a long low building and, each day, the cons were assembled in the prison yard which lay between B Hall and C Hall. They were split into their various sections before they were marched, one group after another, down a pathway to the workshops. Long before Walter arrived, the cons and the screws had named this pathway, with ironic humour, the Burma Road and it was a major part of life in the jail.

During weekdays and nights, when the weather allowed it, the cons played football in the yard. There was also a system of outside working parties and those who had been imprisoned long enough, and who had kept their noses clean, could apply for a place in one of them. As well as squads of painters and stone masons, there were gardening parties who could be put to work, doing weeding and cutting the grass and the like, in the gardens of houses near to the prison. Walter enjoyed the breaks outside the stone walls of the fortress and remembers much kindness from the wives of prison officers who would bring tea and biscuits to the outside working parties.

Walter started in the joiner's shop but eventually got into the stone mason's outside working party, building garages for the prison officers' houses. During the work breaks, Walter would play football – always an obsession – with the children of the prison officers – 'It made you feel as if you were at home with your own kids.' A kindly concession for men who were often hard as nails on the outside but secretly lonely and sick of heart many a day.

Walter, a natural ladies' man, was, of course, starved of feminine company at this stage in his career. But, before his imprisonment for the attack on Mick Gibson, he was doing rather well in the love-life stakes. In addition to Ina, he had acquired a glamorous mistress, in the shapely form of Jean McKinnon. They had met in a bookie's and shared an interest in gambling. Gradually, a desire to fleece the bookie's and show who could really tell winners from losers turned into an affair. Afternoons cuddling at the pictures gradually grew into a more serious relationship. However, it seems that Ina was not too put out by this arrangement. She had her work during the day. Walter was a good provider for the family and seemed to confine most of his canoodling to the afternoons, returning home to play the family man in the evening. Ina tended to turn a Nelson's eye to the situation.

But it made for a bit of fun even when Norval was in Peterhead. He tells it like this, 'One morning I was in the joiner's shop and a screw came in to tell me my wife had arrived on a welfare visit. Ina was pregnant when I was sentenced and she had travelled up to show me the latest addition to the family, Marlene.' How a name for this child was chosen is a bizarre tale. One night, there was a handful of the jail's hardest inmates, including Walter Scott Ellis, sitting around the hot plate. Had a screw eavesdropped on the conversation, he would have had a shock. It wasn't as if the cons were sitting around crocheting antimacassars but the effect would have been much the same. The subject of heated debate was the choice of a name for the new arrival. As well as Scott Ellis, other hard tickets, such as

Banjo Ross, Roddy Mortimer, Eddie Martin and Plum McDuff were throwing their tuppence-worth into the choice of a name for the latest addition to the Norval clan. Various suggestions were made and rejected for one reason or another. Eventually, Marlene found favour among the hard men and so it came about that word went back to Glasgow that the choice of the name for the new wee one had been made.

However, that afternoon, after Ina had left with the baby to head back south, the same screw, who had told Walter of the visit from Ina and Marlene, came down to the joiner's shop again but, this time, he had a puzzled look on his face. 'He told me I had another visitor and I asked who it was. "It's your wife, Wattie," he said, "but this one's a blonde."' It was, of course, the glamorous Jean and she made quite an impact on the prison officers. As she made her way in to the jail, Jean just missed Ina and neither of them had a clue as to how close they had been to meeting in such unusual circumstances. Incredibly, although they had both travelled from the Garscube Road on the long journey north on the same day, their paths didn't cross.

Jean had also given birth – to a son. The 'family' was getting bigger all the time. Ina now had three sons and four daughters and Jean had two sons. For Walter, a man who heard the cell door clang shut on him night after long night, there was the consoling thought that 'at least my women would be kept busy looking after the kids while I was inside' – a thought that would drive the politically correct feminists of today into a rare old tizzy.

But the Peterhead episode was coming to a close and, back home in Glasgow, an era was ending. The destruction of the Garscube Road, as it had been in its heyday, was almost complete. The tenements had almost all been swept away and many of the pubs and shops had closed. The vibrant life of the tenements was draining away as the residents of the area were decanted to new and featureless housing estates. And it was happening in many districts of Glasgow. The well-meaning authorities were providing housing of a far higher standard than that of the old tenements but the new estates offered few of the amenities of the older areas – amenities that had helped build community.

Many of the new housing schemes in Glasgow were to become hot beds of crime with the youths, particularly, joining gangs and making trouble on a nightly basis. The old excuse of 'There's nothing to do here . . .' was trotted out again. There is simply no excuse for teenage violence or dealing in hard drugs but it is also undoubtedly true that, in the sixties and seventies, huge numbers of Glaswegian families were uprooted and transferred to vast areas of modern housing that were without heart or centre.

Take one south-side scheme as an example. Castlemilk was thrown together on the green fields that bordered Burnside, Croftfoot and the little village of Carmunnock, and it was filled with around 60,000 people – the equivalent of the population of a city like Perth. But, when it was first built, 'The Milk' had not one cinema, not one pub, not one library and a swimming pool was something you only saw on television. No wonder that, for a while, 'The Milk' produced gangs of renegade youths creating trouble inside the scheme and out. Older crims returned from the new schemes to create trouble in their old haunts in the inner cities. And gangs of younger men ran amok in the new areas, fighting for turf and attacking each other and anyone who got in their way.

Back in Peterhead, news of such changes to the social face of life in Glasgow filtered in slowly via the newspapers and from the stories brought by wives, sons and daughters who travelled north to visit the incarcerated. Walter felt sick on hearing just how radical the progressive assault on the area, where he had grown up, had become. Lyon Street and his old home facing Scott's had been swept away. He consoled himself with the thought that, if the powers that be had taken away his old road, at least he still had his women.

But there were other surprises to come for Walter on his release from prison. Ina had been given a bigger house, as befitted the size of the family, in the Milton scheme. And Jean, too, had been given a move – to a house just a couple of streets away from where his wife had landed. So a new beginning beckoned for the old Garscube Road villain. He had been moved to Barlinnie for his release in 1966 and there he was met at the gate by a car. Behind the wheel was his daughter Rita who was now a glamorous teenager with her schooldays behind her. Young Archie, too, had completed his schooling and, like Rita, had found a job. The others, Lynne, Geb, Anne Marie and John, were growing up. Even the youngest was walking and talking and ready to give the family a laugh. On his first morning home, Walter woke up in the bedroom and Ina was in the kitchen making breakfast. The toddler looked round the kitchen door and said, 'Mum, there's a man in your bed.' Ina and Walter laughed. The wee one didn't know her dad.

Walter was in a new home, facing a new life in a new district, and poised, as he puts it, to 'get to grips with the money machine'. And to do that he had to write a new chapter on violence, armed robbery and organised crime in Glasgow.

9

ENTER THE GODFATHER

In the late sixties, Glasgow had numerous gang factions, most of which operated on a geographical basis. There was little co-operation between these groupings of men of violence – rather the reverse as much blood was spilled in counter-productive turf wars. Walter Norval, fresh from a stretch in the big house up north, swiftly latched on to this and realised there were rich pickings for anyone with the bottle to organise one major gang. He proceeded to do just that, living, for a time, the life of a sort of Glasgow Al Capone. This was the Glasgow Godfather emerging. Any student of crime in Glasgow is struck by the fact that the major gang leaders, from King Billy Fullerton of the Billy Boys onward, have wrung some reluctant praise from their enemies in police uniforms and on the bench. Had many of these so-called criminal Mr Bigs turned their minds and abilities to honest toil, they would probably have managed to become successes on the right side of the law.

You suspect Walter Norval would have fitted nicely into this group bar the fact that, since he was in short trousers, he had been both a violent thief and a fully paid-up member of the awkward squad. He had a predilection for violence and fearsome rages but this co-existed with a genuine ability to lead. He also had patience, energy and application to give 100 per cent to the task in hand. These character traits formed a potent and dangerous mixture.

He took lawbreaking seriously and liked to think his crimes

through to the very end – even surmising what the potential outcomes, successful and otherwise, might be. In case anything went wrong, he always plotted an escape route. Alongside a conscienceless ability to use fist, knife and gun to get his own way, he had a highly-honed street sharpness. He was a wily lawbreaker who enjoyed planning his robberies in great detail. He liked diagrams and maps of potential sites for robberies which he drew with great care – and enjoyment.

He also had a massive number of contacts, including a huge collection of people who owed him a favour. A lifetime of extortion, thieving, money-lending and gambling had built him the ultimate network of informers in banks, shops and hospitals. If a bank clerk got in over his head with the bookie and needed a grand or two in a hurry, who better to turn to than Norval and his gang? A barman who had drunk or illegally sold most of his stock knew where to turn when a raid on the premises would get him out of trouble. In return for a tip or two, or perhaps the wax the impression of a key, Norval would hand out the readies.

His mistress Jean McKinnon looks back and remembers, as she puts it, that Walter operated a system of 'a tap for a tale' that was handy for anyone short of cash when the rent man or the insurance collector was due. The Godfather paid good money for tips from the grapevine about when and where payrolls were being delivered, news of a van that was crammed with cash and other tasty titbits of information. For a time, this idea of one large gang, combined with careful planning, worked sweetly with thousands of pounds passing through the hands of the gang. Norval's new mob was without a formal name but sometimes they were referred to as the Govan Team. For more than a year before they were finally brought to justice, the city's newspapers featured stories of unsolved bank raids, payroll snatches and the like almost on a weekly basis.

Sometimes, however, this level of 'success' brought its own problems. One robbery on a hospital payroll paid off in spectacular fashion. There were no credit cards or pay cheques or holes in the wall in these days and large hospitals had to pay their hundreds of staff in ready notes. Following this particular heist, the Norval mob found themselves with £28,000 in notes on their hands – a truly massive pot of cash for those days. Nowadays, you'd be hard put to find a branch of any bank with such a sum in its safe. The advent of credit cards, bank transfers and electronic transactions have all led to a shortage of the grubby used notes so loved by the bank robbers. None the less, the considerable sum of cash snatched in this particular robbery posed a problem – the notes were numbered consecutively.

Money laundering was a rough and ready proposition back then and so Walter sent his daughter Rita and squadrons of the family round the shops in Glasgow to buy a packet of handkerchiefs here or a pair of socks there and they always tendered a tenner to pay for something costing a few pence. As they marched in and out of the various department stores with their wads of cash, they made Sauchiehall Street a busy place. Walter remembers one particular store where, every time a tenner was passed across the cash desk, the clerk rang a bell to attract a supervisor who would come over to check that the note wasn't forged and ensure that the change given was accurate. When the Norval family went shopping, bells would go off all round the store in a sort of demented orchestrated tinkling symphony as they and their sidekicks worked to launder the cash.

Some of the same stash was taken in satchels to Ayr races where favourites were backed by an army of money launderers not worried about losing a couple of pounds on a tenner each-way bet as long as the cash that came back was in notes that didn't bear the give-away numbers. With some satisfaction, Walter remembers himself winning £1,100 for one £300 punt and only one of the notes he got back was traceable.

When he was cash rich and, thanks to his conscienceless attitude to thieving, that was often, Walter liked to be generous.

On this occasion, the urge to get rid of the traceable notes led to him throwing the cash around with even more than usual aplomb. After the races, it was fish suppers all round – and a tip of a tenner for the girl who vigorously shook salt and vinegar over the tasty treat before wrapping fish and chips in the obligatory days' old newspaper. Nowadays, that would be like tipping in fifty pound notes – the sort of behaviour you might only expect from a sheikh in Claridge's or the Savoy and definitely not the normal behaviour of customers in a seaside fish and chip shop.

However, if the cash was sometimes distributed in casual fashion, it was always acquired as a result of perspiration as well as inspiration. Part of the success of Norval's methods lay in his patience. He would spend weeks checking out the movements of a payroll van, studying the sequence of the traffic lights in the area targeted and identifying the days when the traffic was quiet so that he could avoid busy spells and possible traffic jams. He made it a rule to rehearse the getaway route thoroughly and lay plans for an emergency abortion of a strike if necessary. Hideaways were chosen for the cars and decoy cars and he even rehearsed what was expected of the gang members when they broke into a bank – even the measure of brutality that might require to be used was carefully assessed.

Such attention to detail led to a three-year spate in which Glasgow's CID were left chasing their tails as they tried to solve a succession of raids on post offices, wage offices, banks and security vans. Guns were a major issue here and they were used as 'persuaders' in many of the robberies. Walter Norval always liked to keep them away from the house and had a secret arsenal of shotguns, revolvers, axes, hammers, knives, swords, masks and gloves in a garage.

The cash flowed in and the sweet life was milked with energy. As kingpin, Walter sported flashy suits, gold and diamonds and fancy cars. There was champagne in the top nightspots and plenty of cash to spend in the bookies' or at the casino which had just begun to be part of Glasgow nightlife. There were also holidays in sunny spots, especially in Tenerife, where the booze flowed and the top restaurants took a pasting. These holidays were generally shared with Jean while Ina seemed content to stay in dull, rainy Glasgow with the family – perhaps she was just happy to be out of the loop of guns and bank raids and maybe, too, she was glad to get a break from a husband who, with the monotonous regularity of bank clerk heading for the office, left home, after dark, night after night, on his criminal missions.

But a life of crime is not without its surprises. And, of course, one day, the police were sure to grasp the fact that the single linking factor in the spate of such cleverly planned robberies was one Walter Norval – the sharp dresser who was leading the good life with cash galore, the Capone of the Cowcaddens. As the net closed on him, Walter took off on another holiday to Tenerife. But there was a surprise waiting for him on his return from the Spanish sunshine. He was met at the airport by the Special Branch and held, along with Jean, for an hour till the Serious Crime Squad arrived. Walter asked why they were arrested. 'Do you think I am smuggling or something?' he inquired. It wasn't until they were back in the familiar surroundings of Maryhill Police Station that he found out that Kotarba, Joe the Pole, had been killed while Norval was out of the country on holiday. He told the officer in charge of the investigation that Joe and he had become friends after his mother had died the previous November and that he had nothing to do with the killing. The officer remarked wryly, 'If that's the case, I wouldn't like to be your friend, Walter.' Until they found the real killer, the police were reluctant to accept that Walter was not to blame. Kotarba's was a death reminiscent of the death of Gacic, that other evil Pole who had come to Glasgow and gone into the prostitution business. One of Joe's call girls, thirty-four-year-old Agnes

Delacorti, appeared in the dock in Glasgow's High Court accused of stabbing him more than twenty times with a kitchen knife in a Maryhill flat. But, after pleading self-defence, she was found not guilty – a verdict cheered in the court. Weeping as she walked free, she said, 'I am leaving this city for good. I had seven years of hell from that man. Now I just want to make a new life for myself.'

She had told the police that she thought that the burly sixty-three-year-old vice-ring boss was going to attack her. This was not a surprising notion considering the sort of man Kotarba was – he ruled his girls with terror and would even amuse his cohorts by torturing them sexually with bottles. 'It was him or me,' Agnes Delacorti said. 'There will be a lot of happy people in Maryhill now he is dead. But none had the guts to do it.' During the trial, witness after witness had revealed to the jury a horrific picture of life in the twilight world of Joe the Pole. The jury heard how his operation, run from his home in Raeberry Street, involved a string of six or seven prostitutes whom he would beat with iron bars and his fists. The court was told how he prowled the streets of the red light areas at night checking that 'his girls' were not cheating on him by keeping some of the proceeds of the sale of their bodies to themselves.

At the end of the trial, Agnes was surrounded by almost twenty friends as she said, 'Everyone hated Joe – I'm glad he is dead'. The newspapers of the time noted that even his stepson Walter Norval had not a good word to say about him. The emergent Godfather said, 'He was a pure animal. He should have been killed years ago.' Earlier, Walter had told the court, from the witness box, that Kotarba had beaten his mother, till she left him, and that, on one occasion, Kotarba had been accused of murdering a girl but that there had not been enough evidence. This was a reference to the prostitute mentioned earlier in this book.

Another witness said Kotarba had stabbed her in the chest on one occasion. And Mr Antone Angel who had shared the flat with Kotarba and found his body described him as 'a horrible man, a dangerous man, a man who could kill. He was cruel and liked to hurt women.' Mrs Delacorti, herself, told the court that the day she killed him he had accused her of 'going with gorillas' – black men. She said that during the fateful last few minutes of this unloved man's life his eyes were staring and she thought that he was going to kill her so she picked up the knife. 'I kept my eyes closed all the time – I didn't know if the knife was going into the bed or into him,' she told the court. At the conclusion of this sad woman's trial, she said that she was going to the north of England with her boyfriend. The night she was released, Walter held a party to cheer her up and 'all the family' were there. And he also arranged for Kotarba's funeral, paying all the expenses, but this was done for his mother's sake. Any notion that Walter was a friend of the Pole was wide of the mark, as the police well knew.

Walter's mother had died suddenly the previous November. She had taken to coming to visit Jean and Walter on Saturday nights in a flat in Willowbank Street that she had provided for them to use as a love nest. They would watch TV, have a bite to eat and a 'wee drink'. If any of the boys were in, she would enjoy a sing-song and join in the fun. Eva had spent her last night alive quietly with only Walter and Jean in the Willowbank flat. She asked Walter to drive her home about 11 p.m. as she was tired. It was raining heavily so Walter asked her to stay but she refused, saying she wanted to go home. Walter took her to her building in George's Road. She told him not to bother getting out of the car and he watched as she got into the lift and gave him a wave. Back at the Willowbank flat, a knock on the door at 5 a.m. proved to be Walter's son Jackie who had arrived to tell him that Eva had only reached her front door when she dropped dead from a heart attack.

After the funeral, she was interred beside her husband Archie and the baby son they had lost. By now, Norval felt he desperately needed a break so he booked that holiday in the Canaries. As mentioned, he was met by the police on his return. Eva had died intestate and Kotarba, as her spouse, had inherited her property and savings. Walter had what he calls 'a talk' with him and it was agreed that they would share her savings equally but that Walter would take the flats and property as they really had belonged to him and his mother. Kotarba was seemingly 'happy' with the arrangement. He had little choice! His old peasant mother's warning to beware of the widow's son turned out to be remarkably accurate.

When Walter had come down from Peterhead after the Mick Gibson stretch, he had been working for bookies. He had also resumed running his mother's flats as, at this point, she had retired and, indeed, he opened up a few more houses for rent. A woman caretaker was employed to keep the places tidy and see that the rents were ready for lifting on a Friday. All this allowed Walter to trouser a fair bob or two and, each week, he also had the brass neck to collect any unemployment benefit, social security and family allowance that was going. He even got £2,500 insurance money after Kotarba's death.

The collection of such easy benefits money, despite wealth from crime, is not a unique trait – that other Godfather, Arthur Thompson, also found the time to milk the system even at the height of his criminal earning power. Maybe the gangsters thought being in the social security loop brought a touch of respectability!

What Walter called the family was, in true Mafia style, growing all the time. He used young thugs, recruited from the Milton and Govan districts, to do much of the violent work but, every so often, he put a bit of his own muscle into the operation to show who was boss. His frightening ability to wield knife and fist and his sheer capacity for fearsome physical violence were constant reminders to make anyone, who had a notion to take him on, think twice.

Although, as has been noted, the planning of the robberies was almost military in its attention to detail, the gang's recruitment operation was to demonstrate a fatal flaw. A man, who was to become one of Scotland's first super-grasses, was taken into the bosom of the mob. Most of the thugs in the gang would bring in a friend from time to time and the circle of gangsters grew almost weekly. A sort of rough-and-ready checking-out went on, to make sure each recruit was fit for the team, but it wasn't rigorous and mistakes were made.

'We were in the Willowbank house preparing for a job one night when my daughter Lynn's husband, one of the gang, brought in a friend. It was the guy who was eventually to grass us all,' says Norval. This was Philip Henry of whom Walter says, 'The first time I looked at him I didn't like him. I said the job that night was off as I had expected another guy, Fred, to join us. My son-in-law told me that Phil Henry was Fred's brother-in-law and that Fred had wanted him take his place since Henry needed cash for a flat.' Henry was wanted for a jewel robbery at the time and was on the run but most of Walter's Govan boys said he was solid and safe. This was to turn out to be a serious collective misjudgement. Henry was admitted to the inner circle of Norval's evil gangsterism and played his role in the splurge of robberies. But, when the law got on to the gang, Henry grassed. Norval's verdict was that Henry was 'a coward – a number one rat, who wanted to do the crime, reap the rewards, but couldn't do the time. He shopped the whole organisation – the men who helped him when he was on the run. How low can you get?'

But Norval's mob had a few more adventures – and a few more close scrapes – before they ended up behind bars. Whispers from the underworld helped lead the cops to the conclusion that, if a Glasgow robbery was carefully planned and successful, the odds were that it was down to Norval and his boys. One breakfast-time raid on a van delivering wages to a hospital almost brought the curtain down on the whole operation. This time, the detectives twigged that the operation had all the hallmarks of some of the early armed robberies and, to check out their suspicions, they headed for the Norval abode as soon as the alarm was raised. But they were a couple of minutes too late at the doorknocker. Walter had arrived home just before the cops and only had time to undress, wrap a towel round himself and splash his face with water, allowing plenty of drips for effect. He denied all knowledge of the robbery and he pointed out that he had just got up, had taken a shower, grabbed a spot of breakfast and was getting ready to face the day. This cockamamie tale, which his wife confirmed, was enough to delay the fateful day when he was finally arrested. Considering his lifestyle, he was fortunate indeed that his wife went along with his tale on this occasion.

During this period, he was leading an astonishing double life. The money flowed in from the carefully planned robberies, which were often executed at night – he was always a creature of the dark. He liked to think of these forays as his 'work'. With this loot and all his other little earners – like protection money, social security scams, rents from flats, money-lending, old-fashioned extortion and the like – cash was not a problem. But, unlike many of the big-time criminals who were to follow in his footsteps, when the law finally caught up with him, he had not attracted attention to himself by living in a flash pad, in an expensive area, surrounded by hi-tech security cameras, with thugs with guns and knives at the door. Instead, he lived in a modest council house in Liddesdale Road, Milton.

At this stage, although he had a record and was well known to the police, they seemed unable to pin him down as the mastermind behind the regular robberies and raids that helped fill the tabloids of the day. The raids were becoming so frequent and were following such a familiar pattern that regular readers of the crime columns knew something special was going on. But, to the outsider, Walter Norval was living the life of a home-loving man with a wife, seven children and six grandchildren. Some of the family stayed with him in Milton, not too far from his old haunts in the Twilight Zone, and others had homes nearby. Few outsiders suspected what was going on. And, by the time he had reached Godfather status and was at his peak as a gangster, his affair with Jean had been running for twenty-four years. The pair formed a deep friendship and the passion and enjoyment of each other's company that they felt have lasted many long years.

Back in his heyday, Walter had a remarkable modus operandi. Most criminals like to vary their movements, to change routes and to keep an eye over their shoulder because the very nature of way they live means that they inevitably garner enemies along the way. Walter acknowledges the danger with a wink and the rueful remark that 'uneasy lies the head that wears the crown' – proof, one suspects, of the value of prison libraries! Routines are dangerous. Studying the routines of wage delivery men and the like was a major ingredient in the planning of the armed raids that were attracting so much attention in Glasgow at the time.

But Walter had a routine of his own, involving afternoons of love-making and gambling in the love nest, in Willowbank Street in the West End of the city, that his mother had provided for the couple. She knew of Walter's long-running affair with Jean and, in an attempt to keep any gossip to a minimum, she stepped in and gave them the flat. And, as has been told, she was to spend most of her last night alive in that very flat.

Most mornings Walter would bid farewell to his family in the Milton council house and pick up Jean from her own home before moving on to the flat to spend the afternoons with her. The cosy domesticity of spending time in their love nest was broken, from time to time, by visits to a nearby betting shop. As night fell, he would take his mistress home and return to his own flat to spend the evening watching television with his wife and family.

However, even during this strange double life, there were some mundane domestic touches in an exotic lifestyle. During the late sixties and early seventies, Walter's daughters Rita and Lynn had married their boyfriends Bill and Danny. The new young husbands were both members of the Blue Angels motorcycle club. Despite not being much interested in cars – other than buying ones suitably big and flashy enough to match his lifestyle and to steal ones fast enough to be of use in his 'work' – Walter enjoyed the bike scene. He went round the bike shows and, with Jean, he took jaunts to the Isle of Man for the Manx Grand Prix. They watched the autumn races round the famous island mountain road circuit – the amateur equivalent of the June TT races. Walter remembers the bikers as 'good lads with a good sense of humour'. In the Willowbank love nest, he'd get visits from the likes of Alan Morrison, John 'Leadbelly' McDermot, his brother Chris, young Davy Heron and many others. The passion for bikes took the lives of a number of Blue Angels in accidents. No matter his faults, Walter is loyal to his friends and he's still close to Blue Angels guys, from back in those days, though they are now 'senior' members. Along with Rita, who is still a biker, he goes to their bike shows and jaunts where he enjoys the company of the leather-clad road burners.

But, in those years, before he was convicted as the boss of the XYY Gang – as police nicknamed his crime syndicate during his trial – violence was never too far away. And those blind rages, which that army psychiatrist identified, years ago in Donnington, describing them as 'homicidal', could still surface. A simple trip to the bookie's could be fraught. Always the snappy dresser, Walter liked to have a bit of style about him – even for a short jaunt down to road to put an ill-gotten pound or two on a nag selected, after much careful study, from that morning's racing pages. He remembers one occasion when his dress for such an outing was a carefully chosen, well-cut blue blazer, complete with shining brass buttons, that would not have looked out of place in a Cowes yacht clubhouse, teamed with neatly pressed light-grey slacks and a pristine white polo neck shirt. His companion, Jean, also wore a blazer and a neat white pleated skirt.

Everything was set for a peaceful hour or two to be spent gambling the afternoon away. But one of the other punters in their favourite bookie's shop either didn't know who Walter was or had been overdosing on the brave pills. This reckless gent remarked to Walter something along the lines of, 'Where have you parked your yacht?' Walter and Jean had left the bookie's and were strolling up the street when the remark began to niggle. Norval had, by now, identified it as a bit of impertinence that could not be allowed to pass. Leaving Jean in the street he turned on his heels, plunged down the road, back into the bookie's shop, and set about the offender with uncontrolled violence. Not for the first time, he was pulled away from a victim by an intervening bunch of onlookers. The red mist had descended and he took some stopping. But he was hauled off the guy who had made such an unconsidered remark. Back in the street, Jean asked, 'What was all that about?'.

'Cheek,' said Walter.

There were other occasions when this tendency to fly into a violent rage emerged. One night, in the Milton Street house, where he now lived, one of Walter's neighbours was taking a breath of air, leaning out of the window, watching this and that, when he noticed a group of four youths making their way along the cars parked outside the house. As they passed, they were scratching the cars, breaking windows and generally vandalising the beloved 'motors' of the residents. These thugs were recognised as a team from another area of the city – a wild bunch who came to the Liddesdale Road area to run with the local youth gang, the Milton Tongs. As the vandals approached

Walter's car the neighbour, who knew just how dangerous it would be to interfere with it, shouted out, 'Dinnae touch that one!'

But he was too late. Walter, alerted to what was going on, was down the stairs two at time. He paused momentarily to snatch a hammer out of the boot of his car. The thugs had scarpered but Walter wasn't giving up. He searched the nearby tenement closes and eventually went to Liddesdale Square – a hunter hungry for prey. This spot was at the centre of the Milton scheme and was where the post office and shops were located. It is also one of the highest points in Glasgow and, today, with many of the old tenements swept away by the bulldozers, you can look from it over to the Campsie Hills with Ben Lomond in the background.

However, on that dark night of bloody violence, it was a very different place. The vandals emerged from a close to find themselves confronted by Norval. One of the young thugs drew out a razor. The red mist descended again. The vandal was struck repeatedly with great force. In fact, so violent was the attack that the head of the wooden hammer was loosened and Walter was moving on to a knife before, yet again, he was pulled off and the fight was ended.

In due course, the cars were repaired in the body shops of various local garages. But repairs on the vandal were a tad more complex as they involved the surgical insertion of metal plates into his damaged skull. He had made a bad mistake in his choice of car to vandalise. And he was lucky that the hammer that came to hand was an old-fashioned wooden one – a steel implement could have killed him. Walter says that incidents like this one always happened as a result of some form of provocation. However, he does acknowledge that the level of violence he has used in response to such occurrences has often been disproportionate. He also claims that he seldom has a clear memory of the events leading up to the outbursts and that he remembers the acts of violence themselves even less clearly.

He might not have had clear memories of his ferocious deeds but others were all too aware of them. Indeed, his ability to spin into almost uncontrollable violence and his unpredictably short fuse were the main factors that helped Walter to ensure that the crime syndicate he had formed round himself would bend to his will. A mistake had been made in allowing Philip Henry into the inner circle but the other members of the organisation were a hard bunch. Walter's two toughest lieutenants were John 'Plum' McDuff, whom he had first met in Peterhead while he was serving time for the attack on Mick Gibson, and Joseph Polding whose underworld nickname was 'The Mallet'. The three of them tended to go everywhere together.

Plum, Polding and others knew that it was Walter, his expertise and tendency to bloody violence that formed the glue that held the syndicate together. And they admired his planning style. When they eventually appeared in court, everyone in the syndicate acknowledged that they depended on the Godfather to mark their targets. One example of his imaginative planning was a bank raid that required a couple of getaway cars. Walter, who had strong but shadowy connections with the Liverpool gang scene, arranged for one car to be stolen on Merseyside and driven north. The car was planted near to the scene of the raid. Also planted in it, in not too obvious a position but still in a place where any cops searching the vehicle would be likely to find it, was one of Walter's maps. Plotted on this was a route from the scene of the crime back on to the M74 – it's purpose was clearly to enable crooks from the south make their escape back across the border.

With the decoy car dumped in the right spot, the gang went on to complete the bank job. When the alarm was raised, sure enough, Glasgow's finest were soon on the scene searching the suspicious car with Liverpool plates. The plant worked. The map was found and, sirens blazing, the cop cars set off across town in a desperate bid to get on to the M74 in time to catch the villains who, they imagined, would now be thundering down the motorway. There were smiles and sighs of relief as the XYY Gang drifted back on to the streets they knew so well and disappeared to lie low for a spell – the cash safely stashed away until the heat was off.

However, the days of booze, cash, girls and gambling and the good life were numbered.

10

FIRE AND JUSTICE

Glasgow, in the twenty-first century, has grown into one of the major tourist attractions of north western Europe. Visitors to the city enjoy art galleries, museums, wide avenues of Victorian architecture and a vibrant pavement café culture. Many will visit the world-renowned Museum of Religion up at the top of High Street, near the cathedral which is, itself, a favourite with tourists. Strolling down High Street and past the old Tolbooth, now a jagged tooth of grimy stone surrounded by heavy traffic but still redolent of the days when it was the centre of city life, is appealing – as are the pleasures of Glasgow Green and the banks of the Clyde.

Opposite the western gate of the old Green, facing the McLennan Arch just inside the Green's precincts, is the imposing structure of the High Court. It is one of the most impressive buildings in the city and has been a prominent landmark since the nineteenth century. The classical pillars of its façade are said to have taken their inspiration from the Parthenon in Athens. Few tourists from around the world, who gaze at it glistening in the sunshine after a £5-million facelift in 2000, are aware that this was an attraction – and a major much-used facility in the fight against crime – that the city almost lost.

One cold and dark night, at the end of October 1977, the city's Central Fire Station received a call from a motorist who, when passing the High Court, saw smoke and suspected that the building was burning down. Indeed, it was. The North Court was engulfed in flames and smoke and sparks were spreading to the South Court. A dozen fire engines and sixty firemen attended the blaze, using turntable ladders and water that was pumped from the then murky waters of the nearby Clyde. The blaze lit up the night sky and could be seen for miles around.

An enduring symbol of the city's fight against crime threatened to disappear, consumed by the flames. But, gradually, the firefighters turned the battle their way and, although the North Court was almost destroyed, the South Court was saved. As is the way with these things, fire inspectors moved in at daybreak. Their conclusion was that the blaze had been started by a deluge of petrol bombs that had been slung in through a skylight. The fires had started on the eve of the trial of Walter Norval and twelve others charged with a series of raids on banks, post office vans and hospitals. The suspicion was that the fires had been intended to destroy a mass of documents and productions that were to be used in the upcoming trial. But, even if the fire hadn't been spotted by that passing motorist, firebombing the court was unlikely to have hindered the trials as all the documents and other exhibits were stored deep in the basement and probably would have survived any fire.

In the event, the trials were postponed for just a few days. Emergency repairs got the South Court fit for use – although, more than twenty years later, lawyers, the accused, court officers and others were still able to look at the blackened fire damage to the North Court. It is now resplendent after the facelift and a multi-million pound extension. Today, visitors can gaze at the sombre building where the infamous Glasgow poisoner Dr Pritchard heard that his fate would be to die on the gallows, just across the road in the Green, in what turned out to be the last public execution in Glasgow. The demise of Pritchard was watched by a crowd said to have numbered 80,000. It was here, too, that Tony Miller, a teenager who was to be the last man to die in Barlinnie's infamous hanging shed, was sentenced. If a motorist hadn't been so vigilant and had the fire brigade not been brave and effective, Glasgow could have lost one of the most important parts of its history. The firebombing of the High Court was to result in a separate trial to follow that of the Godfather and his fellow accused.

So the trial of Walter Norval and the gang of robbers he had so ruthlessly welded together went ahead. His gang were violent men and they were under the spell of an equally violent leader – but he was a leader with the brains to plot the raids which raised the massive amounts of cash they all shared. By studying the contemporaneous reports of the trials, it is easy to get a sense of just how feared Norval was in Glasgow. Lasting sixteen days, the trials were held in the South Court with the ashes of the North Court barely cold and the smoke- and flame-damaged building acting as a constant reminder of the danger of dabbling in the murky underworld of the city.

The court precincts were turned into what could only be described as a fortress. The petrol-bombings were taken as a warning, by all concerned, that those in the dock, and their connections in the underworld generally, were desperate people. Armed police swarmed around the court and the adjacent buildings. It was said that witnesses had been threatened with being shot if they spoke up and some were hidden away, guarded by armed detectives, in secret addresses. On their visits to the court, these witnesses were quickly hustled in and out of security vans so that their exposure to the crowds could be cut to a minimum. And throughout the trials, there was always a crowd at the railings who wanted to watch the comings and goings of this momentous legal circus which had captured the attention of the city and millions of newspaper readers.

The authorities took the possibility of interference with the trials so seriously that the two trial judges, Lord Kissen and Lord Cowie, and the four prosecuting counsel, who were involved in the four separate trials, had to be given special protection. The firebombing of the court had set the official imaginations racing into top gear and there was even speculation that the lawyers involved might be kidnapped or held hostage or worse. Their comings and goings to the court, like those of the witnesses, were carefully orchestrated affairs with the armed guards vigilant and ready to stop any nonsense that might have developed. In the evenings, the lawmen were escorted, under protection, to a city centre gentlemen's club. Once there, the presumption was that not only would they be safe but the menus and claret on offer would be up to the expected standard.

In the court, the public benches were cleared and anyone approaching the precincts was stopped, searched and held until their identity and intentions were clearly established. The journey of the accused to and from Barlinnie and the court was a daily wonder to the citizens who, day after day, read of the exploits of the gang in the papers. It was like something out of a 'B' movie – one that had been directed by a Hollywood hack who had let his imagination run wild. Morning and night, the traffic along the four-mile route from the BarL to the Green was stopped to let a convoy of Black Marias, accompanied by police cars, their sirens echoing around the packed city centre, pass through. And, bringing up the rear, there was an armed support unit to provide that extra notch of security. It was an unforgettably bizarre criminal circus for anyone who saw it. It was also a black tribute to the reputation of Walter Norval and the fear he had created in his native city.

The security arrangement surrounding the proceedings were unique but the trial was also unprecedented in another way. Four different juries heard the cases and Lord Cowie ruled that the accused should not be identified in newspapers or on TV or radio until all four trials were over. So Walter and his associates were merely described in the press reports of the sensational trials as Mr X and Mr Y and so forth. This gave rise to the nickname for them, the XYY Gang, which also had another advantage – it stood out in the big black tabloid headlines when they were convicted.

Thirteen men faced a series of charges in the four trials. The timetable of the trials and the charges show the extent of the Godfather's operation and the cast list along with their fates makes intriguing reading.

TRIAL ONE: Armed raid on Glasgow Savings Bank, Station Road, Milngavie, on 8 October 1976. £2,931 stolen. Armed raid on wages office of Leverndale Hospital, Crookston Road, on 3 December 1976, robbing the staff of £17,035. Joseph Polding pleaded guilty to both charges and another man was found not guilty.

TRIAL TWO: Armed raid on Ruchill Hospital, Glasgow, on 25 March 1977, assaulting staff and robbing them of £390. Found guilty on this charge were Walter Norval, John McDuff and Joseph Polding. Also at this trial: Armed raid on Clydesdale Bank, High Street, Johnstone, on 27 May 1977, stealing £6,120. Walter Norval and John McDuff were found guilty. Three others who stood accused at this trial were found not guilty.

TRIAL THREE: Armed raid on the Southern General Hospital, Glasgow on 1 July 1977, robbing staff of £97. Frederick O'Hara was found guilty and John McDuff admitted the charge. Three others were found not guilty.

TRIAL FOUR: Armed raid on GPO van in Milton, Glasgow, on 8 August 1977 and robbing a postman of £6,715. John McDowall admitted the charge. Four others were found not guilty. Also at this trial: Illegal possession of explosives, including nitroglycerine in a car and in a house in Banff on 28 August 1977. Both Alan Barbour and Philip Henry pleaded guilty. Other lesser charges included on this trial's indictment were: Illegal possession of firearms, including pistols and shotguns, car thefts and damaging hospital telephones.

After such a roll call of crime, it was no surprise that the court handed out sentences totalling seventy-four years. Walter went down for fourteen years and his lieutenants, who, it was said at the time, helped him to create Scotland's first big time crime syndicate, got sentences ranging from twenty-one years to four years. Plum McDuff might have been forgiven for wondering whether that meeting with Norval in Peterhead had been such a fortunate happening – he got twenty-one years. Joseph Polding got eighteen years and Fred O'Hara seven. Alan Barbour, who had admitted possessing the explosives in Banff, got six years. John McDowall got four years and so did the supergrass Henry – this modest stretch no doubt reflected his ability to sing to the authorities about the gang. But Henry also received a sentence other than that issued by the court and his new police friends. Walter Norval swore vengeance and, during his years of incarceration, Henry lived in fear. However, he survived unharmed – a little prison incident involving boiling water apart – and, on his release, he vanished from the Glasgow underworld scene.

As the curtain came down on the security circus that surrounded the trial and with the villains safely under lock and key in various hard case Scottish prisons, the police were at last able to shine some light on the hunt for the XYY Gang. The investigation had taken around a year and involved forces throughout Scotland. Superintendent John Blincow, head of the Serious Crime Squad, was rightly satisfied with his work and told the press, 'Since the team were arrested, armed robberies, which were taking place with alarming frequency in the Strathclyde area, have become almost non-existent and are certainly not on the scale of the previous year. The convictions are not an example of inspiration by any particular police department but they show that sheer routine work, by dedicated police officers of the Scottish Serious Crime Squad, Strathclyde Serious Crime Squad and the divisional officers, throughout Scotland, has resulted in criminals being brought to justice.'

During the almost three weeks of the trials, the various juries heard the police comment on the precision planning and split second timing that had gone into the robberies. Detectives knew, almost from the start, that they were up against their first big-time crime syndicate and that there was a mastermind pulling all the strings. Their big break came when Philip Henry, on the run for jewel theft, was caught and turned out to be a much weaker man than his fellows. He gave the cops much needed information on Norval. This tends to back up a boast by Walter that, in his long criminal career, he was never really caught by the police – only betrayed. Henry's actions still rankle in his memory – as does the recollection that, on one occasion, his own mother 'coppered' him.

The judge's summing-up provides interesting insight into the XYY mob. First in the dock, on his own was Polding, 'The Mallet'. Lord Cowie told him: 'Despite your minor record and the fact that you have no recent conviction for violence, I take a serious view of these extremely serious crimes. They were deliberately executed by you without thought that your violence brought terror to your victims and that you spread terror along with others.'

Polding's counsel, James Farrell, had told the court that the accused was a former shipyard worker. He was a married man with a daughter of twelve. He said that the background of Polding's involvement was that the got deeply into debt with illegal money-lenders who sent two men to see him. According to the lawyer, threats were made to his family and he was told what would happen to them if he did not take part in the Milngavie raid. He was also told that no violence would be needed because a teller at the bank was in on the plot and would hand over the money without any trouble. There was no truth in the statement that any teller was involved. And Polding's share was only £300. It was also claimed that he was forced into the Leverndale Hospital raid where his share was £400. Polding, his counsel maintained, had not taken any part in the planning but was a mere pawn who had taken part through greed and fear for this family and himself.

Next in the dock were Norval, himself, Plum McDuff and Polding again – this time in connection with the raids on Ruchill Hospital and the bank in Johnstone. Lord Cowie told Norval that he had been convicted of two very serious charges both of which had been deliberately planned and executed by him. Turning his attention to McDuff, the judge said that, considering he had been jailed for four years in Chester Crown Court in 1974, he was amazed that the accused was out of prison in time to commit the offences. He told him he had an appalling record. Polding was told that he was to serve six years consecutively with the twelve already imposed.

The prosecuting QC, John Cameron, told the judge that Norval had played an extremely important part in the robberies and, although he was not actually present when they were carried out, he was waiting in a car to provide a second getaway car. Norval, he said, had played a major part in the organisation of the carefully and perfectly planned robberies. And there was evidence that he might have been in possession of a firearm which was actually fired through a door at Ruchill Hospital. That word 'might' in this submission is important and we will return to it later. Lord Cowie ordered the forfeiture of the firearms and a flashy Ford Granada Ghia car in which weapons were said to have been found. The loss of the car still irks Walter as he claims it was owned by his son. This claim was borne out by the fact that, months later, with Norval behind bars, his son, as the legal owner, received an Edinburgh parking ticket for it.

Seemingly, the Glasgow police had gone on an errand to Edinburgh and had used the Granada to get there!

With Walter dealt with, the next up were McDuff and O'Hara. Lord Cowie told McDuff that he had been found guilty of assaults involving girls and young men at the Southern General Hospital. He got another seven years to start at the end of the fourteen years already imposed. O'Hara was told that he had been found guilty of six charges but he, at least, had had the good grace to make a voluntary statement and refused to get involved in other offences. Never the less, the offences were serious and he got seven years. Mr Cameron told the court that the raid on the Southern General had involved smashing a window in the cash office and assaults on three people in the office. One young man was threatened with a hammer and, during the getaway, porters were threatened with a gun. O'Hara was said to be separated from his wife and living with his mother and disabled father.

Last into the dock were Alan Barbour, Philip Henry and John McDowall. Significantly, police kept Henry behind the dock away from the other accused because, as was later explained, he had been put in to solitary confinement for eighty-three days and threats had been made against his life for giving statements involving Norval. Lord Cowie jailed Barbour, who had admitted possessing explosives in a car and a house in Banff, for six years. He then tuned to Henry, who had admitted the explosive charge, and told him, 'You were of considerable assistance to the Crown authorities on another matter before this court'. He then jailed him for four years.

The last man to be sent down was John McDowall who had pled guilty to an armed raid on a post-office worker in Milton. It was said that the accused had attempted to disassociate himself with the violence and he was jailed for four years. The judge was told by Mr Cameron that McDowall had run from the scene when other masked men with him had brought out shotguns and assaulted and robbed a postman. It was said that McDowall had been put up to taking part by a man who had already been in the dock but not on this charge. McDowall's job had been to drive the robbers to the scene and drive them away again but he had taken fright when he saw the shotguns came out and had run for his life. His counsel John Dowdall said, 'The person who put him up to this certainly knew a fool when he saw one.'

Now we'll go back to the supergrass. Mr Roderick McDonald told the court that, after Henry had told the police about Walter Norval and shown them where he had hidden a gun and money given to him by Norval in the Old Kilpatrick hills, threats had been made to Henry's wife. The court heard that, at the time, he was a fugitive from justice after failing to appear in the High Court accused of breaking into a jeweller's shop. He now intended to plead guilty to that charge for which another person had been jailed for three years for his part. Mr McDonald said that any sentence passed on Henry would have to be spent in solitary confinement because of the threats against his life. Mr McDonald said that Henry was in hiding the previous August when his brother-in-law, O'Hara, and Barbour offered to take him on a trip to Banff. He thought, it was said, he was going on a fishing trip and took his rod with him. It was only on the journey that Barbour told him there were explosives in a flask in the car but, stupidly, he carried on.

It took just over an hour to sentence the seven men and, throughout that time, the armed detectives watched inside and outside the building. Before leaving the bench, Lord Cowie said he was deeply grateful to the press for their restraint and discretion in reporting the cases which were of great interest to them and the public – something of an understatement! He now withdrew that restraint and, for the first time, the public, fascinated by a unique trial, found out the real identities of Mr X and Mr Y and company.

11

EXIT THE FRIGHTENERS

Glasgow's reading public could not get enough of the trial of the Godfather and the XYY Gang. For almost three weeks, they had revelled in the unfolding story of Scotland's first big-time crime syndicate. It was as if Hollywood, Capone and Dillinger had arrived on their doorstep on the banks of the Clyde. The adventures of Norval, who had been labelled in some of the tabloids as the 'good-time bad guy', helped the readers forget, for a moment or two, their worries about the mortgage or the poor form of their favourite football team. As if playing along with the public and true to the nature of the film industry, the trial reports ended with a 'trailer' for the next attraction. In the douce, moderated language of the court reports came news that 'following the trial two people – a man and a woman – are facing charges of threatening witnesses who were to give evidence. Another man has already been charged with wilful fire-raising at the High Court building in Glasgow.' For a century and a half, the old North and South courts have been the Old Bailey of Scotland, trying the country's high profile cases. The XYY Gang were behind bars but now it was the turn of their connections to face the spotlight.

In the end, four people faced trial in the aftermath of the Godfather's trial – Rita Norval or Gunn, Billy Gunn, David Garvie of Temple and John McNeil of Govan. The papers reported that it was alleged that, knowing that Walter Norval and others had been indicted and were to stand trial at the High Court of

Glasgow on charges including assault and robbery and contraventions of the Firearms Act, they conspired to defeat the ends of justice by intimidating witnesses. The Gunns were accused of intimidating two detectives in Walter Norval's house in Milton and saying they had a surprise 'of an explosive nature' in store for the police and putting the detectives in fear. It was alleged that William Gunn and Garvie climbed on to the roof of the High Court and set it on fire with bottles of petrol on the eve of the trials of Norval and others on October 30 or 31. Rita Gunn was further charged with conducting herself in a disorderly manner at the High Court on November 2 and putting two detectives in fear of themselves and their families. It is also alleged that, on the same day, she attempted to suborn George Sinclair and his wife Rosemary, both of Maryhill, into giving false evidence at the trial. Further charges alleged that William Gunn and McNeil conspired to intimidate Mr Sinclair to give false evidence at the trial of Mrs Gunn, charged with attempting to suborn the Sinclairs. McNeil was accused of telling Mr Sinclair there was a 'contract' out for him and attempting to intimidate him into absconding – William Gunn was also on a similar charge.

At the end of this second trial, the tabloids trumpeted that 'The Frighteners', as the papers tagged Billy Gunn and John MacNeil, were caged. They were found guilty of threatening witnesses and McNeil got four years while Gunn got five years – basically for telling a Crown witness that 'he would be filled full of holes' if he gave evidence against the gang. Rita Norval and David Garvie, however, walked free. Rita was cleared of intimidating the police and the crown witnesses who gave evidence against her father. That remarkable old Scottish verdict of 'not proven' came into play in the case of David Garvie and the accusation that he had set fire to the High Court with petrol bombs. Rita, Billy Gunn and Garvie were also found not guilty, on the direction of the judge Lord McDonald, of conspiring to destroy the High Court on the eve of Rita's father's trial. The judge told McNeil that he had 'been involved in a very serious charge of uttering threats and putting a person in fear and alarm'. Until now, 'The Frighteners', Billy Gunn and John McNeil, were said to have been just petty criminals.

Throughout the trial, Rita and Billy had held hands as witnesses talked of their fear and the court heard of the threat to fill people 'full of holes'. Rita kissed her husband goodbye as he left the dock to begin his prison term – a romantic gesture, in the Mafia tradition.

The trial had made public the remarkable bond between Rita and Walter Norval. The Godfather might have made many enemies along the way but the love of his daughter has remained steadfast. At her trial, her counsel, Robert Younger, said that 'it was love for her father' that had made her act the way she did during Walter's trial. He told the jury that she may not have been sensible or clever but they were not there to decide if she was sensible or clever – they were there to decide if what she did was criminal or not. The decision was that it was not.

In the great tradition of Glaswegians who 'walk', that is, are cleared of serious charges, Rita gave her side of the story in a series of interviews that were conducted on the steps of the court. It was February and the Valentine she was handed in the dock by Billy Gunn hit the headlines. Billy had made the card in the grim surroundings of the BarL while he awaited trial and one verse read:

> May our love last,
> As time goes by.
> Here's loving you,
> Till the day I die.

*　　*　　*

166

It all resembled something from the lurid pages of an American crime story but with a touch of Mills and Boon romance thrown in. Despite the sentiments of the Valentine verse, that bond didn't stand the test of time and their marriage has now ended but the love between Rita and Walter Norval is still strong.

Rita had been refused bail and, on being charged, was jailed immediately because of the serious nature of the allegations against her. She had spent fourteen weeks in Cornton Vale, the women's prison that lies in the shadow of Stirling Castle, and her observations on prison life are somewhat at odds with that of her father. Cornton Vale was not Polmont Borstal or Peterhead with its 'batter squads' ready to knock awkward old lags into shape. Rita was always highly talkative – indeed, she told the High Court that the police had misunderstood some of her excited ramblings as threats. Of her stay in Cornton Vale, she said, 'The staff were super but, for me, it was still a nightmare. I almost cracked up on my daughter's birthday. The staff tried to be so nice but I missed my two girls so much it was not true.' She was particularly emotional when the prison officers sang 'Happy Birthday' to her. 'I was in prison for fourteen weeks and five days and every day felt like a month.'

On being freed, she poured her heart out to reporters. Here is what she said about her first night home. 'My daughter and I sat on the couch and cried and cried. At night we went to bed together and tried to kid on to each other that we were sleeping.' As dawn broke, she told the press that her daughter said, 'I've been watching you and you have not slept.' 'The Godfather's daughter' was a term the tabloids liked to use to refer to this attractive young woman who was mixed up with the syndicate. But it was a title she hated. She declared, 'The kids are now my main concern. My husband and my father have been taken away from me but they can't take my children. I have nothing else to live for.'

But the nightmare was not completely played out for Rita.

A week later, she was fined £50 for possessing cannabis in Cornton Vale. Joe Beltrami, that Glasgow legal legend, told the court she had been through a harrowing experience. The cannabis had been found on her during a prison-wide search for drugs and Mr Beltrami described it as a 'minuscule' amount. He said she had 'been told that chewing and swallowing this item', which had been passed to her by another inmate, 'would have a soothing and relaxing effect on her.' He emphasised that 'there was no question of trafficking. She had been through a great deal in the last six months.' This was undoubtedly true.

However, even if Rita could now pick up the pieces, her father was still an angry man. To this day, he rages about his trial. The spring after his trial, he went through the ritual of an appeal at the Court of Criminal Appeal sitting in Edinburgh. Herbert Kerrigan QC claimed there had been insufficient evidence for the jury to convict him of his part in the Ruchill robbery but the appeal was thrown out. It was said that forensic evidence had linked Norval and the car with equipment found after the raid. It was concluded that, if he was the one who drove them away from the scene of the crime, he must have known that the raiders were armed. He did not appeal against the other charges, including the raid on the bank in Johnstone.

That his conviction was truly fair is not a viewpoint held by Walter Norval then or now. He makes allegations against the police and questions some of the tactics of his defence team of Joe Beltrami and Herbert Kerrigan. His main accusation is that the police fitted up some of the evidence. Here is how tells it in his own words:

During my trial, a detective inspector, Norman Walker who was known in the underworld by the nickname 'Fit Up' Walker, stated that the Serious Crime Squad found a gun and a cartridge in my car.

What had happened was that, when they took me from

my home, they made me drive the Granada, belonging to my son, to the police station. Walker and the other detectives sat in the car and allowed me to drive. Before we left Liddesdale Road, my son came over to tell them that he would drive as it was his car but Walker chased him away and said, 'Your dad will drive it!' To me, this was to allow them to fit me up and say they had found a gun in the car.

At the trial, in court, Walker was asked under oath, 'Why did you not handcuff your prisoner and you or one of your men drive the car?'

Walker said, 'I can't drive an automatic car.' When asked if he could drive a manual car, he said, 'Yes.' The jury believed this. Why was I, said to be dangerous man, allowed enter a car un-handcuffed and even allowed to drive it when there were several other detectives with Walker – surely all of them drivers. Could none of them drive an automatic which is little different from a dodgem at the funfair? To me, this was done in order that the police could say I was in possession of the car as I was driving it. It was also done, in my opinion, to allow false evidence to be planted – the gun and cartridge. I could not believe that the jury could be so naïve as to believe the police statements.

All those years ago, in Temple Police Station, I accused Norman Walker to his face of fitting me up. He said, 'Walter, you have told lies so I can tell them also.'

I replied, 'You took an oath, on joining the police, to uphold the law honestly not to discredit it. I didn't.'

Regardless of the truth or otherwise about these particular allegations, it is undeniable that, thirty or forty years ago, there was a police culture of planting evidence. One respected figure in the plain clothes force told me, without a hint of embarrassment or irony, that he 'had never fitted up anyone who wasn't guilty.' A curious sort of morality for those charged to uphold the law to the letter.

There were other matters in his trial that provoked the Godfather's ire. Though it has to be pointed out that his appeal was not against all the charges and that what we are dealing with here is ascertaining a correct degree of guilt rather than complete innocence. Walter points out that, during Philip Henry's evidence he stated that he, Norval, had come to his house with guns and he had said this happened on a date when the God-father could easily prove he was in the Canary Islands sunning himself and leading the good life. But the jury believed the supergrass's story.

There was also a mysterious business man who was said to have sold Henry the actual gun Walter claims was planted on him but, despite keeping the man sitting in the witness room for days, Joe Beltrami or Herbert Kerrigan, no doubt for some legal reason or another, did not call him. Beltrami and Paddy Meehan famously fell out despite the fact that Joe, the Great Defender, played such a huge role in getting Meehan out of Peterhead and pardoned for a crime that he had not committed. Walter, soured by this episode, shares some of Meehan's bitterness against the legal profession. Though, as the legion of clever and agile-minded men, who take on the defence of the bad guys, when their day in court arrives, would point out, memory tends to be selective and the victories forgotten more swiftly than the defeats.

When he looks back at the whole dramatic and historic episode of the firebombing of the High Court and the frightening of witnesses, Walter Norval is capable of some shadow-boxing as fancy as any ever performed by his old heroes of the square ring in his Garscube Road days. Asked if he was the man responsible, he falls back on an old ploy of his London gangland counterpart, Mad Frankie Fraser, who, when asked about one bit of villainy or another, tends to give the equivocal reply, 'Well, they blame me for it.' But the court did find Norval guilty enough for his role in the robberies to send him to jail for a heavy sentence. The next day, the tabloids were splashing the black ink around in huge headings – the Godfather was big, big news. The background articles had all been prepared weeks earlier. Teams of reporters had been energetically digging into his lifestyle, interviewing neighbours and acquaintances in pubs, bookies and employees in casinos, gouging out all the dirt they could find on the man who was biggest criminal in Scotland at that time. Walter remembers that, even if the verdict in the High Court had been different, not all of this journalistic effort would have been wasted. One of Glasgow's top crime reporters told him, with a smile, that if, by any chance, Walter had been cleared, as much of the background as the lawyers would allow would still have been printed –with the headline 'The Grandfather' replacing 'The Godfather'!

However there was no doubt in the jury's mind – despite Norval's alleged flaws in the prosecution case – that Walter was bound for Peterhead. But, before he headed off on yet another trip north, he got a shock reading the papers one morning. There was a picture of Alex Ferguson. He is, of course, now Sir Alex and at the helm of all-conquering Manchester United but, at that time, he was the manager of humble St Mirren who play at Love Street in Paisley, not too far from Johnstone where Walter's mob robbed the Clydesdale Bank. The football manager was pictured handing over some footballs to a group of youngsters who had helped convict the XYY Gang by telling the cops about the movements of a car involved in the heist. Walter observes that, perhaps, it might have been better to have helped the lads find jobs rather than dish out footballs to them. These lads had been playing in a wood at Linwood, near Paisley, swinging on ropes in trees when, they told the police, they saw men crossing from the Johnstone end of a river to the Linwood end and entering a blue car which then sped back into town across the Erskine Bridge. This info was important in the hunt for the syndicate – hence the reward of the footballs.

But there was to be a further twist in the tale of Celtic fan, Norval, and St Mirren Football Club. While Walter had been in jail, he had been visited by two of his sons and a St Mirren player and the footballer had borrowed a grand off Walter to go on holiday to the Greek islands. The would-be star was ready to resign at St Mirren and said he would pay back the cash when he did. Walter obliged. And St Mirren did send him a cheque to pay him back. 'The laughable thing,' says Walter, 'is that I was helping a guy whose team had given presents to lads who had played a role in convicting me.'

12

LISTENING TO THE BODDAM COO

In my early days in newspapers and their chronicling of crime, we were under strict instructions, from authoritarian editors, to be very careful about comparing sentences. Judges and Sheriffs are clear on the concept that each case is different and only a trained lawman can decide the appropriate sentence for any crime. Only if you have listened to all the submissions and all the witness and looked at the case in its totality could fair sentencing be decided. Superficial comparisons between sentences for particular crimes were judged to be anathema for the journalist – this was an area the newspaper crime writer should not to be drawn into without taking great care. Earlier in this book, we looked at the apparent inequality involved if a razor slasher was jailed on the basis of a year for every stitch in a victim's face. The cardinal rule is that circumstances alter cases.

However, throughout a long criminal career Walter Norval – and he is not alone among the gang fraternity – has had hammered into him, the hard way, the fact that society seems to have a tendency to hold crimes against property and stealing cash a tad more seriously than crimes such as rape and murder. At least that it is the way it looks to the men who have done long, long stretches for robbery. This curious attitude manifested itself, not for the first time, in Walter's time in prison after the XYY bank robberies.

On leaving the smoke-blackened and fire-damaged precincts of the High Court, Walter took yet another ride up High Street in that familiar Glasgow sight – the dark-blue prison bus with its windows blacked out to stop the curious gazing in at the sweepings of the courts who were heading out east to begin their sentences.

Back in Barlinnie, he was swiftly put into Category A which meant he was classed as a 'menace to society'. And, of course, such status had an effect on his daily life in prison. He was under continual observation and locked up all day except for a one-hour exercise period. This 'exercise' was taken walking round the first landing in circles after the ordinary cons, who were deemed less dangerous, had gone to their work in the sheds. Meals were delivered to his cell and no one was allowed to speak to him through the door. And, just in case someone failed to realise what a menace he was, a huge letter 'A' was affixed to his door.

But Walter, being Walter, had a few cards of his own up the sleeve of his prison uniform. He had many friends in the prison prepared to take the risk of slipping him a morning or evening paper under the door and, on occasion, even smuggle him an illicit cup of tea. Many of the cons he was mingling with had done time with him in Peterhead. Two he remembers particularly are Tony Smith and Billy Fullerton. Fullerton was an offspring of the famous Billy Fullerton, King Billy of the Brigton Billy Boys, the gang leader who had battled with the Norman Conks and Sir Percy Sillitoe and his Untouchables in the thirties and forties. Walter paints an interesting picture of his friends and prison life with the remark that, 'Both lads were 100 per cent genuine cons. The screws would shout to Tony and Billy to get away from my door but the lads would just tell them to fuck off as they were talking to a friend!'

This treatment of Walter had only been in place for a few days when a group of civilians came into the Barlinnie hall on a visit. Visiting dignitaries and groups of people interested in prison conditions are no surprise to the men who live out years paying for their crimes in this jail. It is an antediluvian institution where, at the time of writing, the disgraceful practice of slopping out toilet pails – something that has been discontinued in English jails – was still a daily chore for the inmates of two of the Bar-L halls. (It was finally swept away in Scotland in 2004.) On this occasion, one of the visitors was an MP and he took note, as he watched Walter trudge round the empty, echoing hall, before going off with the official party to study the goings-on in the rest of this massive place. Within minutes a prison officer shouted, 'Wattie, come on down to the desk.' There he asked the so-called menace to society, 'Do you want to mix with the others in the shed and be able to have your meals in the dining hall with your friends?' The question did not need to be asked twice.

It seems that politicians, in those days, had a bit of power. The MP had asked why Norval was being treated in such a way – he was already being punished for his crimes and, therefore, should not be segregated from his fellow prisoners. So Walter found himself, almost immediately, in the sheds with old pals like Barney Noon from Maryhill, Billy Manson and Vinnie Manson. Norval and Billy became particular friends and they stayed that way until Billy's death a few years ago. Indeed, Manson was a regular visitor to the Norval abode and they yarned for hours about the old days in the many prisons they had spent time in. As a souvenir of their prison days, Walter has a large model of a full-rigged galleon that Manson made for him. It is a well-executed piece of work, accurate in every detail and skilfully varnished – the product of countless hours of work. This model vessel has an nameplate attached – HMS *Injustice* which is Manson's comment on the jailing of the Godfather. Other old jail buddies Walter found in the Bar-L sheds included Dickie Bryson and Dunky Bathgate.

But, if the Godfather was expecting a quiet life with his mates in Barlinnie, he was due for a shock awakening – literally. At 6 a.m. one day, his cell door was opened, as he thought, to allow him to go for a wash – but, no. The Serious Crime Squad were at the prison reception, waiting to take him back to Peterhead, the top security prison. All around the landings, the cons banged on the bars and shouted, 'What's up, Wattie?' But you can't beat the system and Norval calmly looked round the hall and shouted to his mates, 'I'm going up north, lads.' It was to be an experience that underlined his belief that society unfairly gave the heavy end of the stick to those who choose to rob rather than those who choose to kill and rape. However, when he ponders these matters, Walter Norval tends to forget his own tendency to violent action.

Within the hour, on a cold dull morning, a convoy of cars had left the East End of Glasgow. The high grim walls of the prison shrank in the rear view mirrors as the police took to the dual carriageways, leading out of the city, and headed north to Perth and beyond. Their destinations were either Perth Prison, Craiginches jail in Aberdeen or the much more feared Peterhead. In one car was a man sentenced for rape and murder. In the other was Walter – a villain convicted of raids on a bank and a hospital payroll. Perth was by-passed, the River Tay crossed and the cars drove into Craiginches.

Norval fully expected that this was to be his final destination that day. His logic was that, since his crime was to steal money, he, of the two prisoners being transferred, was bound for Aberdeen and the murderer and rapist would go to the higher security penal establishment at Peterhead. But it was an assumption and, as I well remember a newspaper colleague telling me years ago, the two most dangerous words in the language are 'I assumed'. And so it turned out for Walter Norval. Incidentally, the belief that society put property and money before life was also underlined to Walter by the fact that, when, back in the High Court in Glasgow, he was sent down for fourteen years, a man in a nearby court got seven for killing a three-year-old girl.

At Craiginches, he was taken and held in one of the cells the cons called 'dog boxes' – cells not much larger than a broom cupboard where there was barely room to sit in the darkness. These horrific and inhumane cells were normally used to contain prisoners who were waiting to be given their prison garb and be assigned to one hall or another in the prison. In this case, the cell was being used to hold the 'menace to society' while he was fed and made ready for the onward journey to Peterhead. Walter was sitting in the darkness in the dog box when he heard a bolt being slid and the door opened. Outside was an old acquaintance – Mr James Frazer.

At this time, Frazer was the Chief Officer at Craiginches. He was a prison officer who had, over the years, won the respect of his charges and earned a reputation as being humane, fair and helpful. He was nicknamed 'Jim'll Fix It' because, like the legendary TV personality Jimmy Saville, he had, on occasion, the ability to make the most unlikely wishes come true. He told Walter that he was bound for Peterhead but that he would rather have him as a prisoner than the murderer and rapist who had arrived in the other car and who was to stay in Aberdeen. Frazer also passed on some bad news to the Godfather. His old adversary, right back to the High Road days, Joe Beattie, who had risen to the top of the CID from the beat in Garscube Road was in hospital with cancer. Frazer said he wrote to Joe regularly and would tell him that he had met Walter as he was en route to Peterhead.

Walter puts it this way, 'Joe and I went back a long way. Him for the law and me against it – opponents who respected each other. Joe Beattie was a fair cop who never stooped to fitting up criminals, planting evidence or any of the other suspect dodges used by some cops.' Jim Frazer agreed to send Walter's respects to the legendary detective who, for so many years, had been such a major player on the Glasgow crime scene and, with that, Norval headed north.

Some of the sights were familiar to an old lag like Walter

Norval and, as the car ate up the miles, taking him from the world of free men to the fearsome institution that was to be, again, his home for years, his mind wandered back to an earlier trip to Peterhead. As the prison bus spluttered along the north-east coastline, an old con, called 'Sheriff', pointed out a prominent lighthouse on the cliffs. 'Do you see that lighthouse? That's the Boddam Coo. You'll hear that howling morning and night. It wakes you in foggy weather and is a nightmare.' The lighthouse was built by Robert Stevenson in 1827 on Buchan Ness near the village of Boddam. Its white light flashes, during the dark hours, summer and winter, once every five seconds and can be seen up to twenty-eight miles away – truly, the lighthouse is one of the sights and sounds of Buchan. With the red and white striped tower disappearing behind them, the old-timer sighed and remarked to his companions, 'Each dawn I die.' Walter says, 'If truth be told, old Sheriff was right. I heard the Boddam Coo howl night after night for many a year.' The waters around Buchan Ness seem to attract dangerous swirling fogs and North Sea haars and the siren, with its mournful call, worked hard.

Walter also remembers that the words Sheriff used, 'Each dawn I die.', were also the title of an old Jimmy Cagney film he remembered seeing. You might imagine that real-life crime and doing real-life time might have turned Walter off Hollywood's fictionalised crime and prison epics but, in fact, he and Jean McKinnon and Rita still enjoyed a TV or video crime-and-punishment film. Were Capone and Dillinger, and the many gangsters that George Raft and Jimmy Cagney played in grainy black and white role models for the young Norval? Who knows? There is a theory in modern psychology that the experts call 'imprinting'. This theory examines who and what might have influenced a person at certain critical times in their development and further analysis of what made Walter the man he is will come later in this book.

During the whole of his prison life, Walter Norval treated the

authorities in a straightforward manner – not for him the touching
of the proverbial forelock or the dropping of 'Yes, sir.' and 'No,
sir.' into the conversation at every opportunity. You call him
Wattie, he calls you Sam or Agnes or whatever. It was a technique
that helped him make some friends on the other side of the
prison bars.

His arrival back in Peterhead showed a human side of the
prison service. One of the officers, recognising him from the
sixties, asked the escort to leave Walter with him, remarking
'Come on, Wattie, you're back home again.' Together they went
straight to the laundry where there was, naturally, another old
acquaintance. This time he was getting reacquainted with a man
called Willie Bennett, aka 'The Wee Red Devil'. This nickname
was no reference to him being an Aberdeen or Manchester United
football supporter – it was much more sinister than that. The
red, in this case, was blood and the prison moniker was an
acknowledgement of the amount of it Willie had spilled on the
streets of Govan on the banks of the Clyde. The Wee Red Devil
was to end his own days by being killed on the Glasgow streets,
outside a pub, by a group of young thugs. But, on this occasion,
he was working in the prison laundry and Walter got clean
sheets, a pillow and a promise that his laundry would get special
attention each week. He was assured that his prison uniform,
towels and bed linen would all be kept in good shape.

Walter was then taken to 'A' Hall and given a cell on the third
landing. It was a bizarre scene. Peterhead had cells full of the old
borstal mates of Norval – yet again more evidence of the lack of
success of that regime in driving youngsters out of a life of
crime. And they gathered to greet the newcomer, bearing gifts.
He was given tea bags, sugar, biscuits, sweets, toothpaste, soap,
shampoo and books – all the things a prisoner needed until he
had earned some prison wages to pay for the little extras. When
jailed, Glasgow criminals take a lot of baggage into the prison
halls with them – senses of hierarchy and humour among them.

Anyone who has watched that splendid movie *The Italian Job* – the 1969 version not the 2003 remake – and enjoyed Noel Coward's portrayal of a Godfather, in velvet dressing gown, pulling the strings of the remnants of his gang still on the outside, gets a flavour of the life of a prison celebrity.

Although there were no cigars or velvet dressing gowns in Peterhead, Norval was still able to be a manipulative figure who managed to get many of the other prisoners to help look after his needs and ease the pain of confinement – a pain that, for many of the prisoners, was assuaged by hobbies like woodwork or painting or writing. One night, the infamous Walter Scott Ellis called his namesake over to his cell for a cup of tea and showed him how he was passing his nights doing marquetry – producing works of art manufactured with inlaid veneers of different woods. This Glasgow criminal legend had a paranoid hatred of the police. His exploits had made newspaper headlines for years and he had eventually been caged for bank robbery, along with his confederates, John 'Bat' Neeson and James McIntyre. Neeson's nickname came from an eyesight problem. Scott Ellis's long prison term meant he had plenty of time to hone his skills for his chosen hobby and he produced items that his fellow cons admired as true works of art.

Over that cup of tea, he asked Walter to pick a scene from one of the magazines that he had on the subject. Walter chose 'The Old Curio Shop' and the other Walter made two versions of it for Norval to send out as gifts. The representation of the old-fashioned shop window was meticulously produced by the convict. Each of the many tiny pieces of different woods was carefully placed in a frame and the end result was lovingly burnished and polished. That was 1977 but Walter Norval still has that piece of marquetry in his possession. Its complexity is remarkable. The shop window is filled with pottery and gifts and an old man, dressed in top hat and Victorian clothes, stands outside gazing in. It is far from the easiest of subjects to portray in marquetry and must have taken an incredibly long time to do. But, as a cynic might remark, being pressed for time was not exactly a problem. From ships in bottles to carving whales' teeth and from sculpture to portraiture, prisoners round the world have always used the long lonely hours of confinement to indulge in and improve any artistic skill they had.

When not discussing matters artistic, the two Walters had much in common to talk about during the long nights, with fog swirling round the prison and the Boddam Coo howling in the background. One person the pair discussed was Norman Walker, the Glasgow detective and Norval's old antagonist. Walker had allegedly told some dubious tales about Scott Ellis in court and helped to get him twenty-one years.

According to Norval, Walker told the court that he happened to have a day off and was in the district where the bank robbery had occurred. He chanced to see three well-known criminals leaving a car and making off. He said he later heard that there had been a bank robbery and, when asked, said the three men he had seen were Scott Ellis, Bat Neeson and John McIntyre (aka Mac the Knife). Asked why he was in the vicinity, he said he had been buying a sheet of glass to repair a window in his home. It all seemed to be stretching coincidence to the limits but the jury swallowed it.

The two Walters would also reminisce about exploits they had on the outside – old scams recalled and picked over in much detail. One discussion they had underlined the ingenuity of the criminal mind. They were talking guns, a subject of much interest to Norval who had some considerable expertise in that area. But even he had to laugh at the story of the gunman who was pursued through a Glasgow park by the cops and had to dispose of a gun in a hurry. No use just throwing it into the bushes or a nearby stream – the metal detectors of the police would soon find it. So this villain climbed to the top of the highest tree he could find and taped the weapon to a branch. When the area was swept with metal detectors, the detectives passed under the gun without a clue to its whereabouts!

When he first came back to Peterhead, Walter was assigned to the tailor's shop which is where the category 'A' prisoners were located until their security status was reviewed and, if they were deemed suitable, they would be downgraded and treated like the other prisoners. One of the old friends he met in the tailor's shop was The Saughton Harrier, Willie Leitch and, as we'll see, the paths of this pair were to cross again later in Walter's sentence. The officer in charge of the tailor's shop was known to his prisoners as Bible John because he bore a passing resemblance to the identikit picture, issued to the newspapers, of the man suspected of killing three Glasgow women back in 1968 and 1969. All three had spent their evenings at the dancing in Barrowland Ballroom, Glasgow. The killings sparked a massive murder hunt that was never resolved. An identikit of the killer was issued to the newspapers and it also featured on television and the hundreds of Glaswegians, who looked in any way similar to the face, were all checked out. This poor Peterhead prison officer had to undergo the humiliation of a visit from the Glasgow CID who were committed to following up every lead – however tenuous. In this case, the prison scuttlebutt is that some of the cons had tipped off the cops about how similar in appearance this officer and Bible John were. Some prank!

The routine in Peterhead was much as it had been during Walter's previous stay there. Each morning, the cons assembled in the yard and marched down the Burma Road to the sheds. The category 'A' men never left the yard until the others were away and they were the last up at lunch and teatime. They were searched as they left the hall in the morning, when they entered and left the yard and also on entering and leaving the tailor's shop in the morning, at lunch and at tea. On an average, they were searched eight times a day. 'I don't think they trusted us!' says Walter.

All this was, according to Walter Norval, yet another example of system taking it out on prisoners who were given, in his opinion, that category 'A' status for lesser crimes, rather than for murder or rape, and they were the ones who had to endure the searches and other irritations. From the prison authorities point of view, it is easy to see that men, who could mastermind a succession of well-planned and well-timed robberies, might be just the sort with the ability and patience to plan an escape. In a prison, where there was a tendency for prisoners to use weapons to attack warders or to force their way on to the roof to pass a happy hour or two throwing slates at those below or maybe even trying to set fire to the prison, the searches were a wise precaution. The violent law breakers who did their time in Peterhead did not have it easy, even if they had decided to be model prisoners, keep their head down and stay out of trouble to get the 'porridge' over as soon as possible.

Walter remembers that, in his cell, there was a red light that burned through the night making reading and sleeping difficult. But, as they say, you can get used to anything and, after a while, the red light was barely noticed. In Walter's prison memories, it is remarkable how even the most difficult of men can settle to a routine. Often this was down to the fact that their individualism, even if this was of a criminal nature, had been ground out of them by a system that can institutionalise all but the most bloody-minded. And, if you have spent large parts of your life in penal institutions up and down the land, the odds are that you will end up surrounded by men of a similar stripe, many of whom would be acquainted with one another. You would also have learned a hundred little ways to make the time more bearable.

One of the secrets of survival in prison seems to be to adapt and make the most of it. One who apparently did that was young John Steele who arrived during Walter's tenure to face a long stretch. According to Walter, 'Johnny Boy', as they called him, had a happy-go-lucky attitude and 'you would have thought it was twelve hours he was facing – not twelve years – the way he handled it.' That was a fellow prisoner's verdict not that of the authorities who found young Steele a considerable thorn in their flesh.

Character judgement can often depend on what side of the fence you are on – in prison and out! But the prisoners themselves were not without compassion. A visitor to Peterhead had shown Walter a photograph of a baby who was dying of kidney disease in an incubator in Glasgow's famous Yorkhill Hospital for Sick Children. He passed it around his fellow cons and they decided to do something to help the hospital. Using their prison wages to buy materials, they started making soft toys and hours were spent on the task until enough toys had been made to fill several sacks. Jean McKinnon and the baby's grandmother collected the toys and took them back to the city to the hospital for distribution to the children in the wards of this huge place. The hospital is a well-known landmark that towers over the north bank of the Clyde. It is famous for its dedicated staff and for its world-class facilities for the care of sick children.

Jean's visits north were regular but the Godfather's glamorous blonde girlfriend, who had enjoyed those sunshine holidays in Spain with him, back in the heady days of freedom before the law caught up with him, had another routine. Every day Walter was in prison, he got a letter from Jean McKinnon. If there was trouble with the post for a day or two the letters arrived in a bundle but, in normal times, they were a daily event. They arrived without fail. 'You can't buy loyalty like that,' he says. In the prison films that Walter likes to watch, the gangster's moll always promises to wait. Usually they don't. Jean did. Walter was not forgotten when the prison gates clanged shut after him. Jean remembered – day after day.

Walter's relationship with his wife was by now a different matter. Ina had never liked it when Walter's criminal life crashed dramatically into her domestic routine. Like Jean, Ina was a hard worker – both women had legitimate jobs to keep them busy while the Wee Mob or the XYY Gang went about their business. Cops coming round to the house asking questions upset Ina. She preferred the quiet life – her work, her children and nights in front of the TV.

Whenever Walter made one of his frequent appearances in court, Ina would sit at home waiting for a neighbour or friend to tell her if he was in the jail again or if he was coming home. Every day, when Walter was leaving the house, he kissed the kids goodbye since there was, as he puts it, no guarantee he would be home for tea, such was the way of life he had chosen for himself. But he did always provide for his family. His kids' early years were very different from his own lonely childhood and, when he was not roaming rooftops or checking out bank deliveries, he was a family man who felt happy and comfortable being with his children. When he was in prison, his wife's rent was paid monthly by what he describes as his 'handlers' and he also arranged cash sums to be delivered at Christmas, the Glasgow Fair holiday and at Easter. Easter eggs for the kids, Christmas presents, wee treats for the holidays – the Godfather made the arrangements.

In Peterhead, after two and a half years, Walter's security category was eased and he got a job in the store room. By this time, he had served five years and been moved to 'C' Hall where there was a better behaved sort of prisoner. Even Walter reflected on the irony of placing him alongside the 'good lads'. For a man who had little experience of gainful employment or the nine-to-five routine, Walter took to the responsibility of his new job in stores with some enthusiasm. The one-time armed robber, who had tortured the Glasgow CID for years with his raids terrorising innocent folk, was opening and shutting the stores in a way that was, for all the world, like a shop owner in civilian life. Every month, he ordered the amount of clothing and stores the prison needed and he got rid of any material that he decided needed to be replaced. This job gave him a bit more freedom to move around the jail and he took advantage of this on every occasion possible.

On one occasion, this freedom even allowed him to do a spot of his old thieving – though on a modest behind-bars kind of scale. The wives of many of the warders at Peterhead would make them up lunches to take in to work – sandwiches or whatever. One of Walter's pals saw a screw open a box of six duck eggs one day and mentioned it to the Godfather who was partial to a duck egg. Walter went down to the cookhouse and acquired two nice hen's eggs and, when the prison officer was elsewhere, he substituted them for two of the duck eggs. Returning from a break, the officer could not believe his eyes. His wife hadn't had time to make him up a piece and he had popped into a fish shop and bought the duck eggs himself. Walter and his pal had a good laugh as the officer stared in puzzlement at the duck eggs that had mysteriously turned into hen's eggs. And they were still laughing as they tucked into a couple of the stolen duck eggs, nicely boiled, at teatime.

By now, Walter had his eye on a move to Dungavel Prison, near Strathaven, on the rolling south Lanarkshire uplands. Too many of those acres are now covered in huge money-generating featureless tracks of forestry but at that time, they were dotted with sheep and cattle and presented an altogether different aspect from the grim fortress that was Peterhead. Here, instead of the mournful lowing of the Boddam Coo, real coos could be seen and heard. In Dungavel, there was also an easier regime with more privileges available. There was even the chance of an eight-hour leave for a home visit, under escort, once a month. But there was a snag. One of the most remarkable pioneers of the Scottish Prison service at that time ran Dungavel. Agnes Curran was the first female governor of a male prison in Britain.

She was a fifty-eight-year-old grandmother when she took up her duties in Dungavel in 1979. It was a medium security prison in these days but, none the less, contained 106 prisoners, 60 per cent of whom were serving sentences for rape or murder.

In her five years at Dungavel (she had previously been deputy governor at Cornton Vale), she showed that a woman can do more than survive in such a tough male domain. On retirement, she said, 'I never forgot that some of these prisoners had been sent to prison for doing terrible things. It was natural that, being a woman, some of them thought they could pull the wool over my eyes or manipulate me but I had been in the service long enough to know when that was happening.'

The use of the word 'manipulate' is interesting and has resonance with regard to Walter Norval and his move to Dungavel. Four times his name was put forward for a move south and four times it was knocked back. When Walter eventually got there, some officers he knew well told him that Agnes Curran had formed the opinion that he was an organiser and manipulator with too much influence over the other prisoners. She didn't want him. With a straight face, Walter says, 'I wonder what made her think that?'

However, the day of his departure was only delayed and eventually Agnes Curran had to face up the fact that Walter Norval was heading her way. The system had ruled that he had qualified for the next stage on the road to freedom. When he was finally ensconced in Dungavel, he told Mrs Curran, face to face, that he didn't think much of her, as a Grade Three Governor, overruling and resisting the judgement of the top man at Peterhead, a Grade One Governor!

When Walter arrived at Dungavel, the infamous Saughton Harrier, Willie Leitch, was already there – as was Joe 'The Mallet' Polding, one of the XYY Gang. Also in residence were Big Jim Roberts and some other Glasgow guys. They knew, from the prison grapevine, that Aggie, as they called her, was unhappy about Norval's arrival and they decided to wind her up. As Walter came out of the van to the reception, The Saughton Harrier stepped forward, deliberately in view of the prison officers, and kissed his hand. The others followed and soon the Godfather was part of a convoy of cons, laden with boxes containing his bits and pieces, heading for the dormitory. He had arrived. The watching officers couldn't wait to race up to the boss and tell her that the cons were paying homage to Norval. That it was all a set-up had escaped the prison officers.

But Agnes Curran *was* right about one thing – Walter was a manipulator. However, she was, perhaps, wrong to fear his effect on her prison and her prisoners. Walter set to work right away to improve things for the cons. Dungavel had been one of the homes of the Duke of Hamilton before it was bought by the Scottish Home and Health department in 1975. The idea was to turn it into a 'half-way' house to freedom. By and large, it worked and the failure rate of prisoners who had to be returned to a normal prison was small. Most prisoners left to freedom or for the open prison at Penninghame, near Newton Stewart, in a beautiful corner of south-west Scotland or to a 'Training For Freedom' hostel.

The inmates at Dungavel slept in dormitories not cells. There were dining rooms and association rooms, a kitchen, medical facilities, a chapel, classrooms and two workshops where the men made chipboard furniture or luggage in conditions as close as possible to that of outside industry. Others worked in gardening or horticulture. There were night classes in basic social education. There were also opportunities for prisoners to do community service and get involved in church work, helping the elderly and fund raising for charity.

But something was missing for Walter Norval, big-time Celtic fan and one time potential football pro – a football field. Well, there was a football field but it had not been used. 'Why?' demanded Walter of the chief officer. He was told that the gardener didn't want the grass messed up. 'I told the chief, "Since when did a civilian decide we didn't play football on our field?"' Walter was fired up enough to threaten to get the cons to write to the prison service HQ, in Edinburgh, with a petition saying they were being denied the recreational privilege to play football. That notion was enough to bring the football field back into play and 'The Great Manipulator' had scored his first goal in Dungavel.

Walter set up games and the lads who could play were allowed outside the gates for an hour and a half of an evening and those who wanted to watch could do so. Eventually, teams from local villages used to come up on Saturdays for a game. The Great Manipulator was now in full stride. To help while away long winter nights, he organised snooker, pool, table tennis and dominoes tournaments. He even put up the prizes – an ounce of tobacco to the winner, half an ounce to the runner up and a quarter ounce to each semi-finalist.

His efforts at keeping the lads interested were contributing to the settled running of the prison but, even at this stage, Walter felt that Aggie wasn't too happy. It seemed as if he was too powerful in the prison and she worried a little too much about Walter and his manipulation. When Aggie Curran retired in 1984, the innovative thinking that had put her at the helm of the jail was deemed an outstanding success. She said, 'I am not a bra-burning, flag-waving feminist but I believe I have done the job as well as any man. In fact, I feel that, because I was a woman, I was treated with far more respect, in certain situations, by the prisoners.'

Despite her gender, Mrs Curran received few concessions from prisoners and staff alike. 'I received a few compliments about my perfume and was often called "madam" but, apart from that, I imagine I was treated the same as anyone else.' Although she had felt the need to stamp her authority on the place – which housed a collection of truly hard cases – she could, when required, employ the gentler side of her nature and frequently wandered around the prison workshops during her five and a half years at Dungavel to see for herself how things were going. And she had a sense of humour. The fact that her successor was to be a man produced the remark, 'Men require equal opportunities, too.'

However, her time at Dungavel was not without incident and she had something of red face in 1982 when a report, by HM Chief Inspector of Prisons, on the state of the kitchens, caused her some discomfort. It said, 'Although the kitchen is adequate for the size of the establishment, it is in need of some repairs. The standard of cleanliness and general untidiness should receive immediate attention.' The problem was soon fixed and Aggie Curran told the press, 'It was a decided embarrassment to me, particularly being a female. I wanted to get my sleeves up and get into the kitchen myself but I remembered my experience in my nursing days that, once you become a matron, you can't go back and do the job of a sister.' The root of this little spot of trouble was the state of the building. Dungavel had extensive dry rot and a leaking roof and the kitchen area seemed to be where the worst of the problems were centred. Tiles fell off the walls and, when the prison service big-wig made his inspection, tradesmen from five contractors were working in the area. With an injection of cash, the benefit of Agnes's organisational skills and some good old spit and polish, the kitchen was soon spotless.

Humour was an essential part of prison life. Indeed, if those incarcerated were to cling on to their sanity a regular injection of it was vital. Dungavel had a more easy-going regime than your normal jail. The report that criticised the kitchen also indicated that, in most areas, the 'half-way-house' concept was a success. The low security rating of the inmates allowed an 'open-door' policy to operate within the Dungavel perimeter. And the Inspector of Prisons, Philip Barry, commended 'the direct involvement of staff and inmates in what is generally accepted as a co-operative venture.' He considered that the prisoners had come to appreciate that the 'relatively new-found freedom, far from being a soft option, imposes responsibilities.'

The freedom to roam around the precincts allowed the prisoners some scope to exercise that essential sense of humour. And our old friend The Saughton Harrier, a man who liked a laugh, took full advantage of it on one memorable occasion. It was not long after Norval's arrival and the pair were working in the cookhouse, dressed, like the chef, in immaculate white uniforms. It was raining heavily – not an unusual occurrence in these green Lanarkshire hills – and Walter and his mate were gazing out of the window, into the yard, watching a civilian worker trying to clear a blocked drain. Willie Leitch noted a large puddle round the drain and said to Walter, 'Watch this guy's face.' Willie walked over to the workman and asked, in a child's falsetto, 'Hey, mister, is that your puddle?' The workman looked at Willie as if saying to himself, 'Here's a real nutcase.' But he denied ownership of the puddle saying, 'No, it's not mine.' At this, Willie dived into the puddle and started to splash around as if he was swimming. The poor workman looked around in anguish, convinced he was dealing with a lunatic. But the prisoners, many of whom were watching this pantomime, were in stitches. The ploy over, The Saughton Harrier calmly retreated to the shower room to change and freshen up. His exploits had given enough entertainment to keep the cons in good humour for a day or so.

Willie Leitch was a first class baker, having spent many years in the trade, before becoming, as Walter says, 'A rascal, like the rest of us.' But he and Norval were soon to be removed from the cookhouse. They were convicted of the heinous offence of giving the cakes they had baked away free to visitors to the prison rather than charging them for the little treats.

Small incidents sit long on the minds of men doing a stretch – even in a 'half-way house'. Always a vain man and very conscious of his appearance, Walter had little opportunity to indulge this side of his character when behind bars. But one small chance did present itself and, like many a man who looks in the mirror of a morning and doesn't like what he sees, he decided to darken the colour of his, by now, greying hair. And, even in prison, that could be arranged. One of the young cons was allowed out during the day to work in Motherwell College's hairdressing training rooms. He brought back the dye and did the business for Walter.

The next morning, when the prison officers noticed the transformation, they told Governor Aggie Curran – altering your appearance can raise suspicions in a prison. A change of hair colour could be interpreted as a good preliminary to a spell on the run. Aggie turned up in the dormitory to see for herself. She arrived in the company of the deputy governor, one of the young rising stars of the prison service who was to go on to rule Barlinnie in his day. As Aggie looked on, the eager beaver deputy said, 'Walter, who dyed your hair?' Always a man able to keep a straight face, the prisoner replied, 'The same guy who dyes yours!' The hairdresser had, for sometime, been looking after the deputy governor's hairstyling – in conditions of some secrecy, of course. Even Aggie had to laugh.

Walter Norval has a pleasant singing voice that has stood him in good stead since the days when his father seated him on pianos to sing the 'John Thomson Song' in clubs and pubs for small change. From borstal to Barlinnie, he had always been able to turn out a tuneful ditty. And so it was in Dungavel. A highlight of the winter there was the annual concert. One Christmas, Walter took over as MC and the cons put on a great show for visitors and staff. The finale was a real tearjerker. Walter spotted a wee girl in the audience, gave her a soft toy, which actually belonged to Aggie, looked her in the eye, from the stage, and sang 'Daddy's Little Girl' just for her. It brought the house down.

The audience at such prison events is always on an emotional knife edge as family and friends share an hour or two with the cons before leaving their loved ones to go back home. They return to the outside world with the clang of locked prison doors and gates echoing behind them. On this occasion, Walter, by now fancying himself as Crosby rather than Cagney, produced the perfect encore. He led the audience in a somewhat maudlin rendition of 'I'm Dreaming of a White Christmas'. Even Aggie Curran was moved. She ignored the loss of her soft toy, a furry animal, and praised Walter and his fellow cons for the best concert ever heard at Dungavel.

But, as usual, Walter had strayed a little – this time, it was just a little – off the safe track. In a show lasting a couple of hours, the busy MC let the words 'Jesus Christ' inadvertently cross his lips when some minor hitch or other cropped up. A committed Christian, Aggie couldn't stop herself from ticking him off for a lapse in standards and criticised him for his blasphemy. You never get 100 per cent!

The whole business of Christmas and New Year is emotionally fraught in any prison. One old lag, who served years in Alcatraz, told me, when I visited the prison island, that the only time he was near to tears during his sentence was when the lights and sounds of the New Year festivities drifted across the darkness of San Francisco bay into his cell. Christmas cards, too, play an enormous role in institutions. The cons produced a programme for that concert in Dungavel with a jolly Santa on the cover. Incidentally, Walter Norval is described in the programme ,with some wit, as *resident* master of ceremonies. And, when in Peterhead, Walter once got seventy Christmas cards at one time. One of these cards he remembers well came from an old con called Barney Noon. On the cover was a candle burning and inside Barney had scrawled:

Walter,
All the darkness in all the world
Can not extinguish the light
From one small candle.
Keep your chin up . . . your old pal Barney.

This, notes the Godfather, was his way of saying they won't ever break your spirit.

Religion has not played much of a role in the life of Walter Norval but he had an intriguing brush with the Church one Easter in Dungavel. A joint prayer meeting was held for Protestant and Catholic inmates. Afterwards, a priest and the eminent figure of the then Moderator of the Church of Scotland went for a cup of tea and a scone in the canteen. A prisoner, called John Pirie, was behind the counter – as were Walter and his old mate The Saughton Harrier, Willie Leitch. Willie took it upon himself to approach the Moderator, the much respected J Fraser McCluskey, and, with a smile, said to him, 'You are the head of all the churches in Scotland – I would like you to meet the head of all the armed robbers!' The Moderator was duly introduced to Walter and the three of them had a wee chat. They all shook hands and Walter was much impressed. In the patois of the Glasgow streets his verdict on the Moderator was that 'The guy was brand new' – high praise indeed.

A Bible that had been given to Willie Leitch by the congregation of Hamilton Baptist Church was passed to the Reverend J Fraser McCluskey who, in a sterling example of Christianity in action, whipped out his fountain pen and inscribed the leather bound and zippered volume, 'To Walter, Willie and Jean, my warm good wishes. J Fraser McCluskey'. Walter Norval has many mementoes of a chequered life and that Bible has a place of honour among them.

13

GOOSE EGGS
AND A GOLDEN ROLLER

As we have seen, in a long career of villainy, Walter Norval has built up a unique body of experience of life inside prison establishments. Early on, he tasted the brutality of the borstal regime. After that, he suffered in the toughest cells in the toughest of military prisons, from Colchester to Shepton Mallet. The massive fortresses of Peterhead, Saughton and Barlinnie were all part of the curriculum in his years of prison education. From the highest security classification to an open prison on the way to freedom, he has tasted and tested all the penal establishment has to offer. And his final days behind bars, at Penninghame Open Prison, near Newton Stewart in Dumfriesshire, left him with more benign memories than those provoked by the beatings and sadism in the 'digger' punishment cells of the old Polmont Borstal or the hard regime of the BarL or the 'batter' squads of Peterhead.

One suspects that his adversary at Dungavel, Agnes Curran, had a hand in his final move. After he had been in Dungavel for almost two years, Mrs Curran approached him to float the idea that he could move to Penninghame. She had a tasty carrot or two to offer to induce the Great Manipulator to move on. If he went right away, he would be in time for a five-day home leave at Christmas. The famous woman governor also pointed out that, if he took the move, there would be a weekend leave once a month. 'I guess she really wanted me out of Dungavel,' remarked Walter.

But the old Godfather was no patsy to be pushed around. He bided his time, saying he would think the move over. It was a no-brainer, of course, considering the time on leave on offer at the open prison. But Walter wanted to make Agnes Curran sweat a little before she could put the kettle on to celebrate him leaving her establishment. On the following Saturday, during the weekly 'inspection', Mrs Curran's deputy approached him. This was Robbie Glen who was to go on to be a governor at Barlinnie (and he was also to become a brilliant and popular after-dinner speaker). Glen was a man with a sense of humour and a straight forward approach.

Tentatively, he said to Norval, 'I hear that you are going to Penninghame, Walter.'

To milk the situation, Walter thought for a few minutes and then replied, grudgingly, 'Yes.'

'Thank God for that,' said the deputy governor. 'You've domineered my prison for the last twenty months!'

No time was wasted. First thing on the Monday morning, the erstwhile Godfather and Great Manipulator of Dungavel was washed and brushed up and loaded into a van raring to start the journey south. His fellow prisoners felt more than a pang of sadness that the man, who organised the football and the snooker and who brought a touch of humour to the prison regime, was leaving. Life would be a lot duller for them. But the staff, from Mrs Curran down, breathed a collective sigh of relief.

Walter's arrivals at new prisons seem to have something of a pattern to them in that there was always an old acquaintance or two waiting to greet him – no matter which jail he turned up at. And it happened again at Penninghame where a group of old mates was on hand to welcome him. And it was also predictable that, since there was a dormitory at Penninghame, known as the anti-social dorm, that would be the place were he would initially be billeted. It was also predictable that this dorm would be well filled with Glasgow criminals.

'So I was amongst my own kind,' says Walter.

And there was to be a curious throwback to the old days at borstal almost forty years earlier. The con in charge of the stores paid Walter a visit. He turned out to be the brother of the young lad who Walter had saved from bullying, by taking on his tormentor in a square go, all these years ago in Polmont Borstal, near Falkirk.

Settled in at the open prison in the south west, Walter pressed his charm and manipulation buttons and set about making life in this, his last prison, a little more bearable. The regime at Penninghame was worlds away from that of the disgusting slopping out and other indignities of the 'big houses' in the cities. But, even in this place, a former country mansion set in acres of attractive countryside, with trees and flowers galore and the River Cree, bursting with fat salmon, running through the grounds, there were improvements a Godfather could make.

Walter arranged for an electric kettle to be provided and for the 'lads in the cookhouse' to lay on a supply of bread, butter, tea, milk, sugar and stuff for sandwiches. This was to be consumed at 'lock up'. Walter ruled these little suppers with a rod of iron. He decided who got what.

One day, a newcomer was attached to the dorm – an interesting character and a man originally on the other side of the law. This was an ex-detective called Gus whose campaigning for animal rights had got him imprisoned. To begin with the cons gave him a hard time, little love was lost between the crims and boys in blue, even one who had fallen on hard times. No one spoke to him. No tea or sandwiches for him.

One of the cons, Billy, had been assigned to make the tea each night and it was his habit to ask Walter who got to share the tea and food. When he pointed to Gus, Walter would say, 'Everyone except him.' But the cons wanted to quiz Gus and find out about life on the right side of the law and curiosity got the better of them. One night, Walter invited Billy to give the ex-cop tea and asked him if he would partake of a sandwich. 'Yes, Wattie, I would like that,' was the reply and, from that moment on, Gus was accepted.

His story was an interesting one. He had left the police after taking against some of the nasty things some of his colleagues got up to. At least that was his story and, in any case, he was preaching to the converted. But it was his belief in animal rights which had pushed him into trouble with the law when, to highlight his protest, he swapped medicine bottles on the shelves of Boots the Chemist with bottles he had adulterated with urine. So it was no surprise then that the cops were after him.

The prison was set in some of Scotland's finest farmland and, with their usual acumen, the prison authorities had deemed that Gus would work in the poultry section and help look after the geese and chickens. Naturally, Walter saw an angle here and soon Gus was bringing goose eggs to the dorm, to be boiled and served on sandwiches. The governor, too, was partial to a goose egg and began to wonder why so few were coming his way. He began to surmise that the old gander was impotent and ordered a younger, more virile bird to be brought in. The idea of losing your 'woman' to a younger 'man' amused the cons. Gus was, by now, assimilated as a convict, and a new gander or not, he made sure that Norval's supplies of eggs continued.

If the food met with the con's favour so did the surroundings. This was a beautiful place and Walter notes that the setting was uplifting. There was a bowling green, tennis courts and country paths that the inmates were at liberty to use for their strolls. The River Cree flowed through the grounds and civilians could be seen fishing its swirling dark waters for the salmon that hid tantalisingly in the pools and eddies. There was even a small lake in which the cons would take a swim of a hot afternoon. This idyll was a long, long way from the dark tenemental canyons of the old High Road in Glasgow. And now, older and wiser, Walter was enjoying it – unlike his last brush with the country life in Lochgoilhead.

Indoor pursuits were also catered for – there was a TV room, a snooker room and a pool room. Inevitably, the Great Manipulator surfaced and soon Walter was running pool and snooker tournaments with entries from the staff, including the Chief Officer, Mr Fisher, with whom Walter got on well. This officer received the ultimate compliment from the Godfather – 'He was a fair guy.' Mr Fisher admired Walter's skill with a snooker cue – after all, the con had been practically reared in the old Tower snooker hall in Garscube Road. Talk about a youth spoiled! But the skills could come in handy and Mr Fisher used to enjoy taking Walter into nearby Newton Stewart to a snooker club where he told all and sundry of the prowess of his man. And, when Walter had seen off the opposition in spectacular fashion over the green baize, he proudly took him back to the jail just in time for 'lock up'.

This humane officer also played a role in a remarkable social episode in Walter's prison life – an unforgettable visit home. His family had set up a surprise birthday party for Jean McKinnon in a hall in Springburn. Jean knew nothing of the party or the part Walter was to play. The prison authorities had let him into Glasgow around 8 a.m. that morning but he had lain low till the party was almost ready to start. With all the guests seated and ready to begin their meal, Jean had her back to the door and he crept up behind her chair. She wondered what everyone was looking at behind her and just as she was turning round he leapt out saying, 'Happy birthday, honey!' and waving a large bouquet of flowers and a bottle of Moët & Chandon. It was a huge surprise for everyone there – especially the loyal Jean. Chief Officer Fisher had played his role in arranging for a leave to coincide with the party and Walter was deeply grateful to him. It showed the humane face of the prison establishment that an old lag like Walter, a man with a horrific record, could be treated in such a way.

That humane face of Penninghame surfaced in other ways. The prison authorities asked for volunteers to help the old folk of Newton Stewart and, on a Saturday or Sunday morning, many went into town to do their bit, being picked up and returned to the prison at 5 p.m. Walter went regularly to the house of an old woman called Anne Howe. He helped her clean the place, made her meals and went out shopping for her. She enjoyed kidding and joking with a street-wise city ladies' man. She was oblivious to his horrifying record of violence and saw another side to this man of many parts. They got on well and, indeed, when Walter told her he was being released and returning to Glasgow she was in tears, telling him, 'Walter, I will never get anyone like you again.'

From Glasgow, the lag used to phone his old friend and inquire about her health and generally cheer her up. She died in 2001 but Walter had paid her one last visit the Christmas before, driving down with one of his sons and a friend who had been in jail with him at one time. They gave her cards and presents and shared an hour or two with her, making the tea and chatting to the old lady who was just out of hospital after an illness. An envelope with some cash for the New Year was left and she waved them off from the doorway. That was the last time Walter Norval saw Anne Howe. She was a 'diamond' says Walter, adding, 'It was an honour to have known her.' On this day out, his companion, from the old days in Peterhead, who helped with the tea and did the dishes, was Donald Forbes, the double murderer – two of Scotland's most famous criminals trying to cheer an old lady up!

Penninghame provided plenty of opportunities for ploys even when the inmates were confined to the jail. The goose eggs were only part of it and, on occasion, Walter would get a couple of chickens brought down from the poultry farm to be cooked for the sandwiches in the dorm or even a used in a curry cooked by a Pakistani inmate called Abdul who the cons called Abie. One night, as Walter played snooker, Abie called in to tell him that the prison officers had found the chickens and taken them to the office. Next morning, as Walter headed to his breakfast, a notice on the board caught his eye. It read, 'Would the owner of the chickens call at the governor's office where they are waiting to be collected.' Screws and cons alike made the most of this with remarks like, 'Why don't you collect your chickens, Wattie?' Walter ignored this banter, after all he still had his goose eggs.

Walter Norval's final weeks and months incarcerated could not be more different than his experiences as a young man in high security prisons. At Penninghame, he ended up working in the Officer's Club – a easy assignment that often saw him whiling away an afternoon in the company of some of the officer's wives who dropped in for coffee and chat. He found them very friendly women who, on open days, would mix freely with the prisoners' families.

And, inevitably, football had a role to play in these final days in jail. He became manager of the prison football team which was often watched by the officer's kids. Walter liked to play around with a ball behind the goals with the kids and always made sure he had a couple of chocolate bars in his pocket for them. It reminded him of life on the outside with his own kids. Walter, surprisingly sensitive about his reputation, enjoyed the company of the youngsters who told their dads they liked playing with 'Mr Walter'. It reminded him, he recollects, of his mother's belief that children and animals can tell by instinct the difference between good and bad people.

In Penninghame, he also worked for a few months at a home, on the outside, for children with Down's syndrome. But this time it ended in trouble. Walter was helping the handicapped youngsters to build a hen house and a hen run and there was no shortage of volunteer kids for his squad – something that irked one of the civilian helpers who was much less popular. One day, one of Walter's group reported to him that this guy had locked a little girl in a wheelchair in a cupboard as a punishment. Walter got the child out and, the red mist threatening to rise again, grabbed the guy by the throat and told him he would throttle him if he ever did something like that again. Back in the prison, after a home leave, he was called to the governor to be told that his services were no longer required at the home. 'Who was the real villain in this episode?' he wonders.

Eventually, when the day came for him to be freed, he went out in some style. He was dressed and ready to go, saying farewell to his friends on both sides of the law, when up came a Rolls Royce – and it wasn't just any old Roller. This one had a gold-plated mascot and gold-plated radiator and bumpers – something truly special. Out jumped daughter Rita with a bottle of champagne in her hand. The cork was pulled and Walter stood in the courtyard with a full glass and raised it in farewell to his prison life and his prison friends.

Later, he was told by visiting friends, who had been in Penninghame at the time, that, for weeks afterwards, the prison officers were saying, 'Who says crime doesn't pay when a guy can serve that kind of time and leave in that kind of style?' It was certainly a question that anyone on the right side of the law might well ask. But, to Walter Norval, Glasgow's first Godfather, being greeted like that on his release was 'just the family's way of telling the authorities that they would never break us and of showing the respect I was held in.' That word again – respect.

On the way home, the party which included several friends from the gangster days stopped at Ayr's famous racecourse, one of Walter's favourite betting playgrounds, where they bought eight bottles of champagne. As they proceeded to drain the bottles by the neck, they were watched by bemused locals who must have thought that some mad pop group had arrived in town.

14

THE SUM OF MANY PARTS

When Walter Norval looked round the Glasgow crime scene, in the seventies, and realised the advantage to be gained by welding together a group of hard and dangerous men into one large well-organised gang, rather that a raggle-taggle bunch of disparate lawbreakers all doing their own thing, he started a trend.

His downfall led to speculation in the press and books of the true-crime variety that, now he was caged, the city would never see his like again. In their book, *Such Bad Company*, experienced observers of the crime scene, respected reporter George Forbes and safe-blower tuned author Paddy Meehan, went further than most. They wrote that 'the spate of armed robberies, which plagued Glasgow month by month, came to an abrupt halt and no organised outfit has, so far, stepped in to fill the vacuum left by the departure of Norval and his boys.' They went on to speculate that it was unlikely that there would be any heirs to his criminal throne. The redevelopment of the inner city, which, in the late sixties and seventies, cut the population there by a third, led to the destruction of the sort of close-knit communities Norval had grown up in. Forbes and Meehan's thinking was that this would lessen the chance of another underworld network forming. It was an unduly optimistic view – Walter Norval turned out to be merely the first of a succession of Godfathers and wannabe Godfathers.

But Forbes and Meehan were right about one thing – the future for big-time crime in the city was to move away from armed robbery – although plenty of that still goes on, albeit not on the scale of the XYY Gang. The future for the hoods lay in marking out territories for the distribution of drugs. As gangsters fought for control of the importation of hard drugs and their distribution, the turf wars that followed were as bloody as any the city has seen. Norval's sinister army of men, masked and gloved and 'tooled up' with the latest weaponry, was replaced by smart-suited men wearing Kevlar waistcoats and not above taking pot shots at each other in the street. The teenage gangs were still running and warring with each other over their territories but the big-time stuff was becoming almost all drug related.

Most observers of the criminal scene in this hard city, in the far north west of Europe, agree that Norval's first successor was Arthur Thompson Senior. Indeed, as we have read, Walter knew him from their days in the BarL and for a time they 'did a little business together'. Thompson, in his early days, was a gangster of a similar stripe to Norval – for both men, extortion, money-lending and the use of force to control their patches were the norm. But, as Norval languished in Peterhead, admiring the marquetry skills of the bank robber Walter Scott Ellis and worrying about the prospects for the next game for the prison football team, the world outside was changing and drugs were now seen as the big money-maker.

Even in America, the Mafia gangs, which had mostly been involved in the numbers rackets, prostitution and protection, were moving into the drug business in a big way. The London mobs, too, were now into dealing and importing drugs to supply their own market and those of the other big cities in Britain. The drugs that flowed into the south east were efficiently moved around the country by a network of hard-men couriers with motorway service stations being favourite hand-over points. The Thompson team had good connections in London liaising with the likes of the Krays and their connections and Mad Frankie

Fraser. Indeed, Arthur Thompson Senior often sent some of his young foot soldiers south for a touch of further education in a criminal 'finishing school' in that other East End on the banks of the Thames. The young Glasgow thugs returned home even harder than they had been and were now enthusiastic advocates for the mega sums to be made in the drug trade.

Arthur's son, Arthur Junior, who was to be gunned down in the street in one of Glasgow's most intriguing and best remembered murder mysteries, was an ardent champion of the new trade – as were various other hoods who had served in the Thompson empire and who were now branching out with 'teams' of their own. It was a different world from that of the XYY Gang and their carefully plotted heists on payrolls and banks. Men, with no conscience, were now selling drugs that promised a lifetime of misery or an early death in some sleazy flat to anyone with the cash to buy. They cared nothing for the damage they were doing to the lives of their customers.

In the immediate years before his death in March 1993, Arthur Thompson Senior, who survived three gangland assassination attempts only to die of a heart attack, swanned around Glasgow. His very presence, at a sporting function or a dinner, brought a frisson of excitement and fear to the event. Usually well-dressed in a dark suit, well-cut shirt and suitable tie, he would inform all and sundry that, these days, he was 'a retired business man'.

There are striking similarities here with his predecessor who now says he, too, is 'retired'. And Walter Norval shares the Thompson liking for smart business suits and he does, indeed, look the part of a retired businessman when he goes on the Caribbean cruises that were his preferred holidays of choice, with daughter Rita and mistress Jean. Likewise, he is equally at home hob-nobbing with the celebrities and watching Celtic take on the cream of Europe at their spectacular Parkhead stadium or buying dinner in a swanky restaurant or nightclub for his many 'connections'.

He still claims to be able to sort out a few problems and do a few 'favours' if required. And that down-to-earth 'I'm as good as anyone' approach, that helped him survive the long years behind bars, allows him to mix comfortably with captains of industry, millionaire nightclub owners or the fans from the terracing alike. But one thing does set him apart from his fellows – on most of his forays around town, he tends to have a serious looking companion in tow – just in case. He has, after all, made many enemies over the years.

Retired or not, he is still able to call in or dispense that favour or two – The Great Manipulator is alive and well and living in Maryhill. When not at the cinema or in front of the telly watching programmes on sport or crime, he is most likely to be found at one of Scotland's racecourses, at Ayr, Musselburgh, Hamilton or Perth, exercising his judgement of horse flesh, a judgement he has built up during his many years of large cash investments on this or that four-legged animal. (Indeed, when the cops first began to get suspicious of his free spending in casinos and on flash cars and the like, he told them the money had come from his gambling winnings. Robbing banks? Who are you kidding?)

He keeps an interested eye on the current gang scene in Glasgow through avid readership of the red-top tabloids that feature the goings-on of the mobs on an almost daily basis – the activities of criminals will always sell newspapers. In the past couple of years, there has been a lot of violence on the streets between warring factions in the drug business. Walter has a special dislike for the drug barons – he dismisses them as little more than shopkeepers. But what is for sale, in these 'shops', is merchandise that kills and enslaves.

However, strangely enough, Walter Norval's last appearance in court concerned drugs. In June 1999, suffering from arthritis, he hobbled from Glasgow Sheriff Court, virtually unnoticed, after admitting possessing cannabis worth £15. The Crown accepted his plea of not guilty in the supply of amphetamine and his defence lawyer told the court that his client, an elderly man, 'was acutely embarrassed about being connected with drugs'. The court was told that Norval was very anti-drugs and was helping a drug rehabilitation programme on a voluntary basis. The court was also told that he had, at one time, 'made banner headlines' but now lived a quiet life and had become a great-grandfather. He was on prescribed medication for the pain the arthritis caused him but he found that cannabis could also help alleviate it. The court reports of this event called him Walter Norville, rather than Norval, but this was no attempt by the ex-Godfather to go upmarket. Not for the first time, one newspaper had made a simple spelling error and others had copied it.

There were other unreported aspects to this hatred of drugs – a hatred that was, perhaps, fuelled by concern for his large family of children from inside and outside his marriage. It is also, perhaps, because he lives in an area where even the most casual passer-by can see vivid evidence of the blight caused by drugs in the many burned-out and boarded-up flats and the shabby youngsters who walk the streets, with drawn faces and unseeing eyes, as they babble incomprehensibly to themselves or to anyone within earshot.

The old crim sometimes takes it upon himself to help, in a freelance capacity, such victims of drug abuse. Neighbours told him of a young girl who lived nearby who was in the grip of a major heroin addiction and suffering beatings from a lout of a boyfriend. Norval took it upon himself to 'advise' the boyfriend to leave both the girl and the area. It was not necessary to lay a horse's head on a bed – a word from Norval was enough. The guy knew Walter, knew his reputation and took the hint. He left the area and the young girl went into rehab. Today she works in an anti-drugs programme.

Sadly in Maryhill, Milton, Possilpark and many other city areas the plight of that young girl is far from unique. There are plenty of youngsters in a similar bind. And Walter's prison experience can help. Another local girl who ended up in Cornton Vale because of a drugs and drink problems received regular visits and cigarette money from Walter Norval. There is no shortage of those needing help. The number of addicts dying from drug abuse in Scotland has risen to record levels. The figures show 382 drug-related deaths in Scotland in 2002 compared with 332 the previous year – a rise of 15 per cent. And the biggest increase was in Glasgow where that total rose from 96 deaths to 126. Most of the deaths involved heroin or morphine. The problem is massive. Government initiatives are being reviewed with regard to treatment and there is speculation that this could lead to more 'detox' clinics rather than the use of methadone which is prescribed as a heroin substitute.

As has already been postulated, perhaps it is worry about his extended family that motivates this great-grandfather's concern about the staggering growth of drug culture. The figures from another academic report show that he and parents and grandparents everywhere in Glasgow have a lot to worry about. Almost 4 per cent of ten- to twelve-year-old children in Glasgow have used drugs and sixty of Glasgow's pre-teen children will have used heroin. Professor Neil McKeganey, of Glasgow University Centre for Drug Misuse Research, highlighted the disturbing case of a pre-teen girl in Glasgow who regularly used cannabis, amphetamines, LSD and Ecstasy and who admitted to using alcohol at weekends. Professor McKeganey said, 'When we look at the age of the children we are talking about, it is shocking. With children there is no such thing as recreational drugs use.' Walter Norval's distaste for the drug trade is strongly felt and he contrasts the damage done to society, generally, by the distribution of drugs with the thieving and fighting of the old gangs. And he is a man who lives, day in and day out, in an area where the damage done by the drugs trade and its importers and peddlers is there for all to see.

But a one-man small-scale war against drugs cannot be used

to condone the actions of Walter Norval down the years. As this book has repeatedly emphasised, the violence, the street-fighting, the use of firearms, the masked raids, that struck fear into nurses and hospitals workers, are acts beyond the pale. And there is no shortage of people ready to condemn his reputation and his life. One famous Glasgow crime reporter said to me recently, as we discussed Norval's career, 'Is he still alive? That evil bastard should still be in jail.' The old Godfather is not fazed by such comments. He knows his reputation and admits to being a lifelong villain and rascal but claims that he never 'hurt' anyone who wouldn't hurt him – all the violence, he maintains, was contained within what he calls 'the business'.

However, there are still plenty folk around, both in and out of blue uniforms, who would emphatically disagree. The fact that the masked man, who is waving a loaded revolver in your face, claims never to have targeted private houses, only businesses, that are well-insured, is of little comfort when your heart is beating in overdrive, your palms sweating and you are in fear of your life. Behaviour like that is not easy to forgive or forget and any redeeming feature in Walter Norval's life story has never impinged in the public perception of the man.

The overarching question, looking back on his long life, is: What made this complex man what he is? A criminal from short pants to grey hair, was he born with evil genes or shaped by life? In short, how does he fit into the nature versus nurture debate that is currently so beloved of the psychologists? Interestingly, his mental condition was never considered in any of his many court appearances which, of course, were before the heyday of mental assessment of criminals – even those who are accused of minor offences.

Nowadays, he would have long periods of assessment of his mental condition and his mind would be examined for the causes of those 'blind rages and homicidal tendencies'. In borstal, as mentioned earlier, he was told he wasn't a hard case – just a head case. And, in the army, that one medical officer, who spoke of both a lonely boy and the 'homicidal tendencies', seems to have the been the only person in authority who took his mental condition into account. The lack of analysis or, indeed, any interest in his mental condition are not of any great concern to him. To him, the path his life took was inevitable for one reason or another.

Reminiscing, in his own armchair, Walter sees only two break points when he could have gone straight and lived a lawful life. One came when he was a teenager leaving borstal. The only praiseworthy thing he had done in his life, up until that time, was to play football well. Everything else had involved aggro and vilification. So well did he play his favourite game, that it was said Falkirk FC were interested in taking him on as a professional. That, he believes, could have changed his life. But it was not to be – the army wanted him, and fast, for his national service and he was dragged south, with the result that the moment, when a life change could have occurred, was missed forever.

His relationship with his mother was complex – indeed, in her haste to take up with the evil Pole, Kotarba, she helped hurry Walter into marriage. And, in his younger years, her devotion to her business interests made him into a lonely child. There was one relative, however, he could talk to – an aunt who listened to him and influenced him for the good. He respected her and took note of what she had to say. But, yet again, those fearsome fists and his temper were to be a problem. His aunt had a son who took to taunting Walter about his hard-man reputation. When they met, his cousin would yell, 'Bow down, here comes God' and the like at him, and it inevitably led to that old Glasgow solution to many a problem – a 'square go' in a back-court. The fist fight didn't last long. Walter broke his opponent's jaw with the first punch – a blow so strong that his companions recall that the crack of bone was heard through the close-mouth and out in

THE SUM OF MANY PARTS

the street. After this, his aunt never spoke to him again and another exit route to normality was closed.

Looking back, he also remembers that, once you develop a reputation as a hard man, a leader of the pack, it is difficult to step back into the shadows. Up front, as a leader of a gang or a man with a reputation, you can't show weakness. And you are continually tested by wannabes trying to knock you off your perch. Your actions get harder and harder to sustain your position and the violence escalates. In the language of the old Western films Walter used to watch, there is a new gunfighter in town every day – an adage that applies just as strongly to the High Road and Glasgow's tenement canyons as to the High Plains and creeks of the American west. You have to see the challenger off to maintain status and respect. It is an interesting theory and one that gets some validation in research which has resonance in the life of Walter Norval, particularly his boyhood. Material from the Edinburgh Study of Youth Transitions and Crime, co-authored by Professor David Smith of the School of Law at Edinburgh University and Dr Lesley McCara, shows that 'early encounters with the police may leave a lasting mark on children who are labelled "the usual suspects" and can not shift the tag when they grow up'. The study found that boys are much more likely to be involved in violent offences 'but this appears to be part of "a normal expression of masculinity" for teenagers'. Youths who have committed offences are also very likely to become victims of crime – and, likewise, youngsters who have had offences committed against them are more likely to offend.

This long-running study, which featured in the *Sunday Herald*, also has some interesting observations on gang membership. About 800 youths interviewed said the group they spent time with constituted a 'gang'. Of these, 150 were in an organised gang – defined by researchers as a group with a name, a saying or a sign. Members of these gangs were typically male from broken families and of lower-class backgrounds. They were more impulsive, more likely to take risks and more ready to admit to being involved in criminal behaviour. One of the main conclusions of the study's report called for a policy to give youths a bigger stake in their communities.

This is a powerful report on youth crime in Scotland but psychologists and academics around the world have been involved in a long-simmering row about the influence of nature and nurture in criminal behaviour. It is an intellectual slugging match with no clear victor, so far, and there is unlikely to be one in the future. Walter Norval's life fits in with many of the conflicting theories on offer – he offers fertile ground for those trying to come down on one side of the argument or the other. There are several important features from his youth: after the death of a father, who was frequently absent, his mother largely left him to fend for himself; his selection of Foy and O'Hara, the Kings of the Garscube Road, as his major role models; the frequency with which he observed violence at first hand; and being brought up in the overcrowded conditions in the tenement homes of Garscube Road.

Famous research by Konrad Lorenz, in the thirties, centred on the concept of imprinting. This is a phenomenon which can be observed most readily in birds, especially ducks and geese. Lorenz had noticed that, in the absence of the mother bird, a newly hatched duckling or gosling will assume that the first live creature it sees is its mother and will immediately form a lifelong social bond with that creature. His studies helped to validate the belief that there is a very strong predisposition to *imitate* the behaviour of those around us. For a young person, a role model is very important from a very early age. If this is correct, it makes Norval's choice of Foy and O'Hara, whether deliberate or by chance, highly significant. And other role models for the Godfather-to-be, like Dan Cronin and Evil Jim Kemp, add to the theory that you can 'imprint' and attach yourself to disastrous

212

people whose influence brings out the worst in you. The Lorenz theory postulates that we have a genetic predisposition to form attachments early in life and, like ducklings and goslings, we will turn to whoever is available for us to imprint on. And, as we have seen, the folk that Walter Norval came in contact with – the ones he could potentially imprint on – were mostly a bunch of violent lawbreakers. In his case, the lack of regular attendance at school and the absence of any authoritarian figure in the form of a teacher or someone such as a church minister to offer guidance, were, perhaps, significant factors too.

There is some resonance, too, with the social interaction theory of James Tedeschi and Richard Felson who think that even hostile aggression might have some rational goal behind it – for example, severely punishing any provocateur in order to reduce the likelihood of future provocations. This rings true in the case of Walter Norval who explains the level of violence he used in street fighting as a young man by his belief that, if a battle started, you hit back so hard that there was little chance of an opponent coming back for more of the same. It is also the case that, in the days of his youth, most of his potential opponents would carry a razor or a 'blade' – as he did himself. The 'square go' was a different matter – combatants knew the rules and would largely stick to them. But, in street fights and in pubs, the broken pint glass, the knife and the razor were commonplace. Some street fighters wore their criss-cross, stitch-marked facial scars with pride. It was almost as if the ugly purple weals acted as badges that denoted toughness.

Walter, who survived mostly unmarked, apart from losing a small piece of his ear which was bitten off in the Gibson back-court fight, views it differently. He tells of one old acquaintance on the High Road who had 'a face with as many lines on it as a street map'. Walter saw this not as a mark of hardness but merely as confirmation that this 'bampot', as he called him, had 'never won a fight in his life'. Clearly, the violence Norval saw as a very young child, looking out of the tenement in Garscube Road on to the streets and pubs below, had an effect on the man he became. The canal-side bare-fist fights, the battling of gangs, the random violence of a pint glass smashed on a pub counter and plunged cruelly and bloodily into an opponent's face – all this was part of the experience of living in a culture where, more often than not, might was right.

The overcrowding of the tenements was also a factor. Looking back, many of those, who lived their early years in tenements, talk of the close-knit sense of community, the attitude of 'we are all in it together so we had better help each other'. Much of this is romantic nostalgia and nonsense. The overcrowding and the lack of adequate sanitation or heating are pushed to the back of the mind. We are told that the summers of old were endless idylls of sunshine and blue sky but the spitting sleet and biting cold of sub-zero winters in unheated Glasgow tenements are never mentioned.

Incidentally, there is ample evidence, in the annals of psychological research, that, if humans are subjected to overcrowding, the propensity towards violence increases, just as it does with animals. There is recent evidence, too, that seems to favour the view that a predisposition to violent behaviour can be inherited. The *Guardian* science editor, Tim Radford, reported on a study that suggests that two New Zealand scientists, working at King's College, London, and the University of Wisconsin, Madison, have found a gene that may play a role in the cycle of violence and the extent of its inheritability. A deficiency in a gene called MAOA had been linked to violent behaviour in previous studies but, until this study came out, the evidence for it had not been presented convincingly. The New Zealanders studied 442 boys of whom 154 had been mistreated in childhood. By mistreated, the scientists, according to Radford, meant that they 'had either experienced sexual abuse, beatings or rejection by mother or foster parents'. Of these 154, fifty-five were found to have a less active variant of MAOA and the other ninety-nine had the more active variant. These fifty-five were, Radford says, 'more than twice as likely to have been involved in antisocial behaviour than the other mistreated group. They made up 12% of the total, but were responsible for 44% of all crimes committed by the entire cohort of 442 young men.' From this, it can be concluded that there is substantial evidence to support the theory that, for people with a certain brain chemistry, the exposure to violence or abuse in childhood can be the catalyst that will send them on the way to becoming violent adults.

One of the most intriguing bouts in the nature-versus-nurture debate is between two big-hitters. Steven Pinker, Professor of Psychology at Massachusetts Institute of Technology, made waves with his book *The Blank Slate*. In it, he claims that the 'blank slate' is, in fact, a myth. The book claims that 'the doctrine of the Blank Slate may have done more harm than good. It denies our common humanity and our individual preferences, replaces hard-headed analyses of social problems with feel-good slogans, and distorts our understanding of government, violence, parenting, and the arts.' The tendency to behave more violently or less violently than those around you is innate and the type of parenting you have makes very little difference. He believes that siblings raised in the same family are no more likely to resemble each other in nature than they are to resemble children outwith their immediate family.

One of Pinker's fiercest critics is clinical psychologist Oliver James whose book, *They F*** You Up*, argues exactly the opposite. Basically, James believes that children, who are born to violent parents but raised in peaceable households, are no more likely to end up with criminal records for acts of violence than those born to non-violent parents. However, those raised in homes run by violent adoptive parents tend to be criminally aggressive. Academics are, therefore, divided about the causes of violent behaviour but it seems likely that both our genes and our environment, at least to some degree, have their parts to play in our propensity to aggression. This argument on nature versus nurture, the cerebral equivalent of the canal-side slugging match, goes on. You pays your money and you takes your choice.

An examination of the life of Walter Norval, through which he has written himself into the city's criminal history, can offer some insight into the argument – but on which side is a moot point. There are those, of course, who don't like to highlight the goings-on the underworld of Glasgow at all – even in the context of learning from it. There are those who, figuratively, pull the blanket over their heads and pretend the culture of gangs, with their attendant violence, doesn't exist now and, what's more, never existed in the past – or, if it did, it has been overemphasised and sensationalised by newspapers and TV stations.

Plenty of politicians and a few right-leaning leader writers take this view and suggest that Glasgow has an undeserved reputation as a hard city. From the days of Alexander McArthur's twenties' novel, *No Mean City*, onwards, those holding this view have squealed when some of the patently undeniable nastiness of the city is exposed in a book or in a newspaper article or, especially, in a TV programme. Every major city has an underworld and an ugly underbelly. Glasgow is no exception. But no problem can be solved if its existence is not admitted. That a new Glasgow has emerged over the last few years is true. That the Glasgow of Walter Norval existed and exists is equally undeniable. That there are underworld drug wars still going on is also an uncomfortable fact of life.

An examination of Walter Norval's life and his world is not without value for a city willing to learn from its past. To question what made this particular citizen the man he was, and is, is both interesting and valid. It is a question that should not be swept under the carpet.

The nature-versus-nurture theories and the rash of recent physiological examinations of what makes a criminal produce complex arguments. And Walter Norval is a complex man. He's a man without conscience about his crimes but a man who believes he lives to a code – it's just that his is a criminal code that's pretty far removed from the rules of ordinary society. But it is a code he believes he never breaks. It is the sort of code that made one of his old Peterhead companions serve long years for a crime he did not commit rather than rat on the man who did. It is the sort of code that leaves Walter Norval still, all these years later, brimming with hatred for that supergrass Philip Henry. And it explains why he's still searching for the once-trusted lieutenant who broke the code and sent the XYY Gang to jail. It is the sort of code where 'respect' is everything and where the praise of your peers is vital. It is the sort of code that acknowledges the existence of the bent cop and the detective, who will twist the rules, and, yet, on the other side of the war between the law enforcer and the law breaker, it also recognises that there are 'straight and fair' cops.

And, where prison officers are concerned, Walter Norval has also seen and suffered the violence of the sadistic 'screw'. He has also seen the kindness and humanity of some prison officers, their wives and families. For his own part, he has dispensed much violence and spilled much blood and, in the process, made many enemies. There are many Glasgow citizens still around with memories long enough to recall Walter Norval and his reign of violence. And they despise him and all he stood for.

It is said that every man is a sum of many parts. In the case of Walter Norval, that should read many, many, many parts – extortionist, violent armed robber, money-lender, gambler, lover, family man, criminal planner, storeman, landlord, lonely child, motorcycle buff, streetwise kid, prison expert, enforcer, practical joker, knifeman, wages clerk, bookie, gang leader, street fighter, cartographer, footballer, sports fan, anti-drugs campaigner, getaway driver, father, grandfather, great-grandfather and GODFATHER. And more. What weight should be put on each of the many parts of this man and his intriguing life? That is for you to decide.

INDEX